# The Music In My Life

An inside look at entering the difficult world of being an
opera singer when past the age of 40

By

## Betty Jones

This memoir is dedicated to both my parents,
Mary & Bill Powell
who brought me into this world of the arts.

To my children, Jeff & Janet plus grandchildren
who bring me joy
each and everyday of my life.

and
most of all to my husband of 60 years,
Eugene "Doug" Jones
without whose love & devotion, my career and
book may never have happened.

Library of Congress ISBN# 978-0692335574

Cover designed by Sumner Jules Glimcher

# Chapter Index

# Prelude

In all honesty, I never really envisioned my becoming an opera singer. After marrying, I only thought of myself as a wife and mother, the more traditional role for a young woman in the early 1950's. I had been an art major in college but also enjoyed singing. Luckily, shortly after getting married in 1954, my husband and I moved to Wilton, Connecticut, where I continued my art work in a newly constructed combination studio and dining room. I soon joined the Wilton Congregational Church Choir and eventually became their alto soloist. This exposure paved the way for me to be cast by a local theater group to sing the role of Madame Flora in Gian-Carlo Menotti's *The Medium*, my very first venture into the world of opera. The whole experience proved to be surprisingly enjoyable. I decided then and there to see how far I could go as a singer.

The Congregational Church Choir Director, recognizing my nascent talent, arranged for me to sing for a former Wilton resident, Georgiana Gregersen. She was a well known voice teacher at the Mannes College of Music in New York City. Evaluating my sound, she said: "Your voice is very beautiful, but you don't know, technically, how to sing! ---- I would like to teach you, if you can come to the city once a week for a lesson." Needless to say, I was both pleased and surprised by her comment. When I hesitated, she added that I would become one of her scholarship students. My smile broadened as I thanked her and answered, "Yes"

After several years of intensive study with Georgiana at Mannes and then with her teacher, Gibner King, my voice grew upwards into the soprano range, while still maintaining its alto richness on the bottom. Besides teaching voice, King was a skilled pianist who, in his day, had accompanied many famous singers, including Ezio Pinza. Gibner and I performed many successful concerts together for various organizations in Connecticut and New York. At one concert, Paul Kwartin who sang with me in *The Medium*, was amazed at my more dramatically expressive upper register. His many connections with various prestigious music organizations made him a very valuable friend. He suggested I enter the Concert Artists Guild Award Competition.

Although I was well past the age requirement for the competition, I, never-the- less auditioned, was accepted, and won the 1969 Concert Artists Guild Award. The coveted prize was a New York debut at Carnegie Recital Hall on March 25th 1969. A review of the concert appeared the next day in the New York Times. The headline read: "ENTHUSIASTIC HOUSE HEARS BETTY JONES."

## BOSTON OPERA:

Because of my New York concert success, I was for the first time regarded locally as a soprano. The new choir director at the Wilton Congregational Choir asked me to become the soprano soloist in the Church's annual holiday performance of Handel's *Messiah*. Linda Cabot Black, one of the founders of the Boston Opera Company, had recently moved to Wilton and happened to be in the audience for this Christmas performance. After hearing me, she arranged for an audition with Sarah Caldwell, the Artistic Director and Conductor of the Boston Opera Company. As a result of this audition and Linda's generous recommendation, on March 12th, 1971 I made my professional opera debut in Boston, at the age of 41, singing two small roles in Charpentier's *Louise*.

## SAN FRANCISCO OPERA:

Good news travels fast, and In the fall of 1972, I made another exciting debut with the San Francisco Opera Company, singing the roles of Woglinde and Ortlinde in Wagner's complete *Ring Cycle* alongside the legendary soprano, Birgit Nilsson as Brünnhilde and Thomas Stewart as Wotan. While I was in San Francisco, the head of the Seattle Opera

Company, Glynn Ross, evidently had a telephone conversation with Richard Rodzinski concerning a production of _Aida_ Ross was planning, for the grand opening of a newly built Civic Center in Phoenix Arizona. He was looking for a soprano to sing the title role. Rodzinski, who was the assistant to the General Director of the San Francisco Opera, had heard me sing during rehearsals and concluded that I would be a perfect Aida. Ross flew down from Seattle the next day to hear me. I did not know the role but, luckily, had studied one of the important arias, "Ritorna Vincitor" from Act I. I sang it for him and he immediately engaged me. Ross insisted, however, that I report to Seattle the day after my final Ring performance of _Götterdämmerung,_ and begin preparing for my first leading operatic role.

## FIRST AIDA:
Once I was in Seattle, coaches worked 10 hours a day teaching me the role of Aida. The only time I stopped studying was at mealtime or to sleep. A major role generally takes many months to learn and I only had three and a half weeks. The long awaited opening of the Phoenix Civic Center was quite a glittering event. President Nixon's Daughter, Tricia, cut the ceremonial red ribbon and Arizona's Senator Barry Goldwater was the Honorary Chairman. To add to the festivities, the Annual Governors' Conference was being held in Phoenix at the same time. Governors from all 50 States, including Thomas Meskill from my home state of Connecticut, were in attendance.

Since Aida was my first major role, I will always be grateful to Glynn Ross, Conductor Henry Holt and all the wonderful coaches at the Seattle Opera for their patience with and faith in the then unknown soprano.

During my career, I sang many additional Aidas and other leading soprano roles, including Tosca, Turandot, The Countess (_Le Nozze di Figaro_), Leonore (_Fidelio_), Amelia (_Un Ballo in Maschera_), Senta (_Der Fliegende Holländer_), Odabella

(*Attila*), Abigaille (*Nabucco*), Eva (*Die Meistersinger*) and Rezia (*Oberon*). I sang in Europe and Australia and with major opera companies and symphony orchestras throughout the United States.

## CONNECTICUT ARTS AWARD:

The crowning moment of my totally unexpected career occurred when the Connecticut Commission on the Arts presented me with its coveted 1986 Arts Award at a "black tie" dinner celebration. A 30 minute television special on my life was shown on Connecticut Public TV throughout the state. Past winners include the celebrated contralto, Marian Anderson, fellow Wilton resident jazz pianist Dave Brubeck and the noted historian Barbara Tuchman.

First "Aida" with Seattle Opera Co. (1972)

# Early Days

As I look back and reminisce about the "music in my life," I think about how fortunate I was to have over the years been in the right place at the right time. How did all this start? Let's go back and see.

## THE BEGINNING:

The magic genie seems to have granted my every subconscious wish starting with the first word I imagine I heard jarring me awake. It was --- "Push!" I slid out of my tight but comfortable quarters and was instantly picked up by my heels and slapped on my back. I let out a loud musical cry, which echoed throughout our Plainfield, New Jersey house. After all I had never been formally introduced to this gloved guy. How dare he slap me so!

My cry ricocheted off the walls in the bedroom of our three-story white wooden house (looking just like all the others on the block) in an Irish/Italian neighborhood. The year was 1930 and my family were the first people "of color" to live there. As is their custom, the Italian/American mothers came to welcome and congratulate the new mother. They all agreed --- "She's-a-gonna be an opera singer. We can hear her all the way down-a the block."

How was I to know that "Push" was to become the basis of my operatic technique, eventually making it possible to sing leading roles at the New York City Opera, Seattle Opera and Chicago Lyric Opera, be a member of the Metropolitan Opera Company and perform all over the world.

## THE FAMILY:

My parents were an American amalgam of races: German, Irish, Cherokee, and African-American. William I. Powell, my father, was tall, slender and light skinned, with a profile that

5

resembled the Indian on the old five cent piece. Mom, who was born in Guyana (formerly British Guiana), came to New York in 1920 at the age of 15 and became a U.S. Citizen. Later in life, when my parents traveled in Italy, the Italians thought my Mom was Italian and spoke to her in their language. Likewise when they were in Mexico, everyone thought she was Mexican.

Early on, from the moment I slid into home plate, I was aware that our house was always filled with music. Mom held me in her rocking chair and sang to me as I nursed at her voluminous breasts. She had a lovely mezzo voice and had studied piano in her youth. As I grew older, she became my first accompanist, the first person with whom I sang duets and a staunch creative supporter.

Dad was a mechanical engineer who worked for the City of New York when Fiorello H. LaGuardia was Mayor. He commuted daily to the City by train from Plainfield. He was part of the design team for the then new Sixth Avenue Subway and the Delaware Aqueduct Tunnel, working for the New York City Department of Transportation and for the Board of Water Supply, respectively. Musically, he had an untrained bass voice and taught himself how to play as Fats Waller did, "stride piano" by ear, but only in the key of C. If Dad was not jazzing it up on the piano or working in his vegetable garden, he listened to records of his favorite jazz pianists and symphonies played as loud as possible.

Laughter is spasmodic singing. They use the same muscles. One can always spot singers by the richness of their laughter. Occasionally, after a meal, Dad and I told each other funny stories and    laughed until we cried. We had even more fun making music! To capture and save our musical moments for antiquity, Dad went out and bought a recording device. It recorded on soft plastic discs that had to be played with a cactus needle and the needle was sharpened on a circular emery board. I still have tapes recorded from those original discs. Dad was the first person to record me singing.

My Dad's father, called Poppy, was known as the "King of Fun", so my funny bone may be an inherited characteristic. He was born during the 1800's in Maryland, and at the age of 90 he could still jump up in the air and click his heels together many times before landing.

I learned about the Civil War while resting on Poppy's knee. He said he was once sitting on the side of the road when an elegant carriage approached. A man's head emerged from the window. Poppy said, "He was the ugliest man I'd ever seen and he was wearing --- a stovepipe hat." Yup! It was Abraham Lincoln.

Poppy studied and taught music, played the piano and organ and conducted church choirs. He was gifted with perfect pitch. One of his students was Mary Saunders Paterson, who later became Marian Anderson's first voice teacher. An elegant and dapper man, particularly in spats, he was an expert in dancing the "cakewalk." Poppy formed a group of traveling singers bearing his name. They were called "The Powell Jubilee Singers" and sang light opera, including Gilbert and Sullivan's, and spirituals all over the United States.

**Poppy's Powell Jubilee Singers (1882)**
**(He is seated at center)**

I wanted desperately to write down some of my grandfather's stories but alas, I did not know where or how to begin. After all, at the time I was in the third grade.

On most sweet summer evenings, Mom, Dad, Poppy and I would all rock on our front porch and sing hymns and spirituals in harmony. If a rocking chair had moved forward a foot with each back and forth motion, we would have traveled many miles every summer.

Poppy lived to be 97. In his last years, his speaking and singing voice became a wisp of its former self. Most people are unhappy when they catch a cold, but that was not true of Poppy. When he caught a cold, he delighted in his newly found voice. The effects of his cold evidently caused his voice to regain the power and resonance he delighted in during his prime. Poppy's "Good Morning" at breakfast caused all our heads to turn towards him, as having lived another day, he smilingly beamed at us triumphantly!

**Celebrating Mom & Dad's 50th Wedding Anniversary (1976)**

## EARLY ENTERTAINING:

If friends popped in unexpectedly or were invited formally, I felt a rippling tingle of excitement. "Aha," I'd say to myself, "Now I'll have an audience to entertain." In our living room, I carefully set up the chairs in rows and ask Dad to play one of his classical records so I could dance for them. Sometimes I asked Dad to play jazz on the piano, then I would sing. My favorite was:

> Hot ginger and dynamite,
> they have it every night,
> Back in Nagasaki,
> where women chew tobaccie
> and a wickie wickie wackie woo!

Thank goodness for an audience made up of friends. They always smiled and clapped enthusiastically, no matter how they secretly felt about our performance.

My need to perform was met more formally when the teachers at Emerson Public Grammar School decided to delve into the works of Wolfgang Amadeus Mozart. I was chosen to play the part of his sister. It was lucky I had been studying the piano since as a part of my acting role, I was to play a simplified version of a Mozart air. Mother made my costume, a full length pink dress with lace at the neck and panniers at the hips. I loved every minute of the rehearsals and the actual performance. Group pictures were taken of the integrated cast in costume. I was so proud to be a part of the cast. I was to again perform Mozart in the future, and in costume, but not until my days at the New York City Opera.

## OTHER GRAMMAR SCHOOL HAPPENINGS:

Suddenly one summer day in Grammar School, the boys discovered me. I was bending over at the drinking fountain in the hall when I was startled by a quick kiss on the cheek by one of my male classmates. The boys began to tease me unmercifully on the playground during recess, but I could take care of myself. Dad always secretly wished he had had a son.  I partly fulfilled his wish by learning how to defend myself, fly kites, sail toy sailboats on park lakes and build an apple basket scooter on roller skates.

When I was in the fourth grade, one boy in particular made me angry enough to haul off and kick him in his unmentionables.  His friends carried him off the playground. I felt two emotions, surprise and sorrow.  I later apologized to him.

At the sound of the school bell one afternoon, I decided not to use the aisles between the desks and chairs, but rather to hop over the furniture to get to the classroom door and home the quickest way possible.  I may be the only girl who has lost her virginity to a chair.  When Mom did the laundry that week, she must have seen the blood in my underwear because she questioned me about it.  I told her the truth. "Yeah Mom, I hopped over the chairs.  I must have hurt myself." She asked more questions and finally took me to a doctor.  I guess she did not believe my explanation.  Before I knew it, I was hauled out of the Emerson Public and put into St. Bernard's, a Catholic School.

## ST BERNARD'S CATHOLIC SCHOOL:
The Catholic School was only a short walk away from the public school I had attended --- but --- what a world of difference between the two. One big difference was that I was the only person of African-American lineage in the entire school. The enrollment at the public school had included many children of color.

The dear sisters in their black and white habits tried their best to control and civilize me, but I had other thoughts.  They were given the right by parents to act as guardians while children were in school --- including administering a slap when they deemed it necessary.  I learned early on to duck so the wall behind me was punched instead of my getting slapped. "Ouch!

It was usual for the kids on our block to call each other out to play by whistling, but, for some reason, I could not whistle even though I tried and tried! All that came out was a faint sound and lots of air, so I taught myself to sing in the whistle range, "YOU HOO-oo!"

Another clever but annoying trick Dad taught me was whistling in my throat. No one could figure out where the sound was coming from. When the teaching sister finally figured out that it was I, she pointed to the coat closet and said in a very stern voice, "Betty Powell! go sit in the cloak room and don't come out until I tell you."

Little by little, however, the sisters recognized early on that I had a superior voice. I was both intrigued and lucky when a retired opera singer was brought in once a week to give group lessons, held in the building adjacent to the church. These turned out to be my very first voice lessons. A choral group was formed to sing at masses. Later while in high school, I came back to conduct the group.

Besides music I was also irresistibly drawn to the visual arts. I would spend hours whittling a large cake of Ivory Soap into shapes I fancied.

I asked Dad for an art book so I could learn to draw the human body. I soon began to copy in pencil the nudes from the book and quickly the art entrepreneur in me was born. At home, I copied the nudes and then brought them to school the next day to sell to the boys for five cents each. Because of the excitement that seemed to suddenly surround me, the sisters quickly sniffed out what I was up to. One day, something told me to empty my notebook of these drawings. Sure enough, the sister thought she would make an example and called me up to her desk in front of the entire class. She said, "And bring your notebook!" I obliged, but her face fell when she found absolutely nothing but my school notes.

The mother superior and the other sisters must have had a conference about me because, from then on, I was asked to decorate the top of the blackboard with pastel sketches of flowers. I was in seventh heaven since I had permission to draw during classroom hours. Time was officially set aside at St. Bernard's so other students could also draw for the first time.

## SISTER RITA CLAIRE AND SISTER ANGELA MARY:

Of all the Nuns who taught at St. Bernard's, two stand out in bold relief and I shall remember them forever. Sister Rita Claire and Sister Angela Mary wore black habits and stiff corrugated white material framed their faces. A black scarf covered their heads and below they wore a black blouse, black skirt, black stockings and thick-heeled utility black shoes. From their waists hung a beaded chain holding a large silver and black crucifix.

Imagine for a moment a cold, snow-covered winter afternoon. I was sledding on my father's Flexible Flyer which he had bought as a child with money he earned by delivering papers. I slid back and forth in front of our house. Growing tired of the monotony and always seeking new adventures, I finally "belly wopped" down the street and around the corner to St. Bernard's Church and School. I saw Sister Rita Claire and called to her, "Hey Sister, can I take you for a ride on my Dad's Flexible Flyer?" I was stunned speechless when she said, "I'd love to." So with her black habit flying in the wind, she settled down on the sled and held on tightly. I grabbed the towing rope and down the block in the middle of the street we went. As she slid by smiling, the kids cheered, clapped and jumped up and down.

Sister Angela Mary may have looked just like all the rest of the sisters in their habits, but a closer look betrayed a distinct genetic edge. She was unforgettable because she peered through two entirely different colored eyes. One was blue and the other brown. I never dared try any of my cut-up, attention-getting tricks in Sister Angela's eighth grade class. Although she was always warm and smiling, to her, teaching was a serious business. We learned a lot under her tutelage and she loved all her students en masse and individually. The last day of class before graduation, her disparate eyes shed copious tears. She knew she would miss us greatly. I was touched by her tears.

Over the years, I kept in touch with Sister Angela. When I made my debut at the New York City Opera singing the leading role of Amelia in Verdi's _Un Ballo in Maschera_, she came to hear and support me. After she retired, I, in turn, took my accompanist on several occasions to Convent Station, New Jersey and did complete programs for her and the other aging sisters at their retirement home.

**St. Anne Villa**
**Convent Station, N.J.**
**April 29th, 1997**

13

**St. Anne Villa**
**Convent Station, N.J.**
**April 29th, 1997**

# Teen Age Years

## LIFE IN PLAINFIELD, NEW JERSEY:
Back in the 1940's, Plainfield, New Jersey was prejudiced against people "of color," and the city was harshly segregated. For example, there were two YMCAs and two YWCAs, one for whites only and the other for blacks. We had to sit upstairs in the balcony of the local movie house, and certain restaurants were forbidden to us. Social customs at that time dictated that the black and white races be kept separate, particularly in social situations. "There was to be no intermingling," Mom would repeatedly explain to me when I was in high school. If I happened to bring a white classmate home, I would be reminded, "Dear, she is your school friend only."

Because I was light-skinned and had blondish hair, I generally could sit or eat anywhere I wanted. Most whites were not aware of my connection to Africa, of which I was very proud! Blacks looked at my facial features, read my heritage and then nodded, smiled, and, although they were perfect strangers, greeted me warmly. Segregation causes a group that is marginalized and despised to be especially loving to one another and therefore very strong. After all, they are all brothers and sisters who have been rejected.

## INTRODUCTION TO DANCE:
While doing the dishes one day, Mom was startled by a loud crash emanating from somewhere upstairs. She looked up at the ceiling, then rushed up the stairs to see what had happened. Mom found me slowly getting up from the bedroom floor. "What happened, Betty?" she breathlessly asked. "Oh Mom, I was walking down the hall from the bathroom and tried to go into the bedroom when my foot got caught on the frame of the doorway." My mother decided then and there that I should study dance so I would

begin to move with more feline grace and this kind of accident would never happen again.

Mom knew of dance classes being given at the Men's YMCA (the Black Men's "Y," which was located in the segregated, rundown section of Plainfield). But, how was I to get there? We had no car! Mom called her friend Harold Doré, the owner of a black cab company to drive me to the "Y." Harold did not send an ordinary cab to take me but instead sent a stretch limousine with a plush fur carpet on the floor. I felt like Cinderella at midnight! With or without the limousine, I learned experience in dance is a necessity in the performing arts. Dance classes at the "Y" were the start and cornerstone of my future theatrical life.

Most major opera houses have apprentice programs to familiarize opera hopefuls with the various elements needed to play a convincing role both musically and dramatically. Movement in opera is a stylized art form. Thanks to Mom, I learned at an early age that studying dance puts one in touch with the entire body. Every movement a singer makes in a performance is calculated to enhance the credibility of the character being portrayed. Singers who are not in control of every fiber of their bodies and who are under pressure to perform show their nervousness in many strange and unconscious ways. This can include repeatedly clutching a piece of clothing and all kinds of inappropriate body movements.

## PLAINFIELD HIGH SCHOOL:
Plainfield High School was a large brick building with many windows all the same size. It overlooked a small verdant park. High school was for me a glorious time of growth. I not only reached almost six feet in height but I began to paint, sculpt and study voice seriously.

I joined the Plainfield High School Chorus. Thank goodness the director taught voice privately, for under her watchful eye

I began to study my first operatic aria. It was a mezzo aria in French from the opera _Carmen_, called the "Habanera." She also taught me diaphragmatic breathing. I felt weirdly embarrassed when she pressed my hand against her overweight middle as she took a breath to demonstrate how I must learn to inhale when singing. All babies and small children naturally breathe from their lower gut. That is why they are shaped like tadpoles. Their rib cages are so small that they cannot possibly breathe in their upper chest alone. At sometime in their lives, however, they begin to breathe up in their chests, perhaps because they are slumped over a desk at school for hours at a time or just plain bad posture, Unfortunately, it doesn't make for good singing.

Before long, the chorus director assigned me a solo part in a concert, the first of many. In the darkened high school auditorium, as I was taking my bows in the bright spotlight, I made out my father's hands held high above his head. While the rest of the audience clapped with loud enthusiasm, Dad noiselessly alternated slipping one hand the length of the other over his head as if he was washing them under running water high in the air. I could not decide how to take this silent applause. Was it approval or disapproval?

The ego of an artist is fragile, a tender green sprout. The garden of humanity in which it grows must be kind and encouraging with just the right amount of loving sunny support. What is flowering in the artist's heart and soul must be allowed to come out unhindered, although with guidance by someone more knowledgeable in the arts than the artist. Hence the artist studies with someone who has "been there and done that" on a professional level.

Mother made it her number one priority to make sure I got voice lessons. She received a small monthly allowance from my father who I doubt made very much money working for the City of New York. Somehow she husbanded their resources, sewed in my aunt's dressmaking shop and scraped together enough money to pay for my lessons. I don't think Dad knew about this until much later when I was a sophomore at Sarah Lawrence College. I had sung excerpts from *Porgy and Bess* in a staged production. Dad was dumbfounded. He exuberantly clapped and clapped and at the end rushed up to speak to me. "Where did you learn to sing like that?" he smilingly asked. "I've been taking voice lessons." He questioned, "Here at Sarah Lawrence?" "No, all along when I was in high school." He was incredulous. He turned to Mother for clarification. "Yes Bill, she's been studying all along. You knew, didn't you?" That was the end of his noiseless clapping and also the end of his endless teasings.

## JEWISH COMMUNITY CENTER:
To get to Plainfield High School, I had to take a #18 bus into the center of town, then walked further to school. After school one day on my way back to the bus, I heard interesting music wafting from a building like the delicious aroma one experiences when passing a really good restaurant. I followed the sound. A sign over the door read "Jewish Community Center." I went in and was quickly surrounded by welcoming, warm people and was encouraged to join in the singing and dancing. It was there that I first danced the Hora and learned folk songs both in Hebrew and Yiddish. As a young prospector in the music field, I had struck a vein of gold, because people of the Jewish faith were to mentor me intermittently throughout my life.

I enjoyed my daily walks past the Community Center. I would slow my pace so that I could listen to what was going on inside, like a bird cocking its head while listening for the presence of a delicious worm. On one particular occasion, the convergence of time and space left an indelible imprint on my memory. As I slowed down to stand still, I felt something quite hot between my breasts. What a strange sensation! I pondered its presence. The "hot something" slid down my chest and pooled in my belly button. What was it?

18

How did it get there? I quickly scurried across the street and ducked into the sheltering privacy of a closed store's entrance. Turning my back to the street and grabbing a hankie from my pocket, I proceeded to wipe between my teenage orbs. Down further and further I went until I reached my belly button, successfully cleaning out the last vestiges of an unidentifiable substance. The time had come to discover the truth. Was it animal, vegetable or mineral? Eventually I concluded that a high flying bird had chosen me as his bombing target. He fixed me in his crosshairs and "bombs away." I was so stunned with curiosity that I did not have time to be revulsed. Since then, I have felt that the whole happening should be viewed as a blessing. From then on, good luck followed me wherever I went.

## MESSING UP IN A PERFORMANCE:

What do you do and how do you feel when you mess up in a performance? On one occasion, the high school chorus director accepted an engagement for the chorus to sing at the Plainfield Library Festival. We were all dressed in our Sunday-go-to-meeting best bib and tuckers. The audience quieted down expectantly as we were given the signal to rise to our feet. The concert proceeded and finally we heard the familiar piano introduction to our last piece and prepared to jubilantly burst forth in song. I was supposed to sing the solo part accompanied by piano and chorus and I had studied it well --- or so I thought. As the music moved along measure by measure, I became more and more nervous. Adrenalin was coursing through my veins. I managed to sing a few notes before I drew a complete blank, gave up and sank behind the chorus and burst into tears.

After that experience, I was determined it would never happen again. Negative thoughts before you sing spark the "flight-or-fight" syndrome. Once they get started, there is no way to stop them. Under the stress of performing, the mind usually remembers the melody even if the words escape one. The Germans thought up a unique way of solving the word problem. They sing over and over "Die swarze katze lekt ihm am arsch" until they remember the real words of the text. In English, the translation is "The black cat licked his ass."

I have learned from experience that the most important thing I can do for myself is to plant a positive seed in my mind long in advance of a particular performance. It generally will germinate, flower and bear fruit so that the gaping mouth of the stage-fright monster, Tyrannosaurus Rex, won't have me as his main course. I usually say to myself, "Just have a good time!' If one aims for that, the audience is bound to have a good time, too. No matter what goes wrong, one must always show love for the audience. Whatever the jagged rocks and pitfalls of a performance and even if one stumbles or dashes one's foot, as long as the audience believes the performer loves them, all will be forgiven.

## DATING:
Dad never bought a car. He felt that having a garage on our property would sacrifice some of his much loved vegetable garden. If I was invited to a party of my friends and could not beg a ride, Mom would take me by bus. This sometimes required many hours of traveling. During the party, she sat in the kitchen and hoped for a ride home. Mom always made sure I met and socialized with the "right" people.

Dad's unique form of ridicule ascended to its peak of perfection when I began to date. I think there was an element of jealousy in his changed status, as he now had rivals for my time and attention. When I was a baby he named me "Walliber" because that was the sound I made when I was crying, "wa-a-a-lib." When I studied dance at the Black Men's YMCA, he called me "Tapper." You guessed it -- I was learning how to tap dance. In pubescence, I was "Nin-com-poop." As I grew tender swellings on my chest, I became "Nin-com-poopa-teets." As the years passed, his name for me became longer and longer ultimatatly culminating in the tongue twister "Nin-com-poopa-teets-a-rye-zink-a rye-zonk-a-rizer."

Since I was my Dad's buddy, he actually cried when he heard that I had experienced my first menstruation period. Mom said knowingly and wisely, "Bill, she's been your sidekick for all these years but --- now my troubles begin." She feared the possibility of an unintended pregnancy.

My favorite swain at that time was Victor. He was light skinned, a mixture of black and white, and his family came from the West Indies. Victor, who lived in a Bronx apartment with his parents and sister, had to board many a train and subway, plus ride the ferry across the Hudson River, to come visit me in Plainfield, New Jersey. If for some reason transportation failed, he would ride his trusty bicycle all that distance, even crossing the river on the George Washington Bridge,

Most Black people of a certain social standing in the community know each other. In the 1930's and 40's, we as a race were not welcomed into white society. Various organizations of every description were closed to us. This was especially true of country clubs. To counter this, the West Indians of color in the New York area wholeheartedly enjoyed the relaxed warmth of their Karma Social Club. I remember smiling faces beaming from fast fading black and white group pictures taken at elegant luncheons in large halls. Almost everyone knew everyone else and could name their forebears back a few generations. Victor's family knew my Mom's family, so he was given the stamp of approval to date me after a formal introduction.

What I loved most about the Karma Club were the exotic accents of its members. Each Caribbean Island sported a slightly different accent. I enjoyed studying them all and tried to imitate them. I knew I had succeeded when one of the Karma members asked me after we had been introduced,

"Which Island are you from?"

## EARLY OPERA EDUCATION:
Early on, I was baptized into the Richard Wagner music cult by my father. He loved to play and listen to records (turned up to zenith volume) of the Wagnerian sopranos of the past, principally Kirsten Flagstad and Helen Traubel. These voices were of monumental volume and rich in timbre. They were mezzo-sopranos with surprisingly beautiful high upper register extensions. Their dramatic voices encompassed two registers in one voice, mezzo and soprano.

Dad did not seem to care much for Italian operas. He thought the tremolos sounded like the siren when a police car sped at breakneck velocity to a crime scene. It was Victor who introduced me to Italian opera. He had bought many records of his favorite tenor, Richard Tucker, and delighted in sharing them with me. He even sang along quietly with Tucker.

As for me, when my career took form years later, my experience with the Wagnerian sound helped me to better understand the leading roles I was cast to sing, namely Senta in *The Flying Dutchman*, Eva in *Die Meistersinger* and several smaller roles In Wagner's complete *Ring Cycle,* which I sang both at the San Francisco Opera and the Kennedy Center's Washington Opera.

## HIGH SCHOOL GRADUATION:
To the stately strains of "Pomp and Circumstance" by Elgar, the soon-to-graduate class of 1947 Plainfield High School graduates lined up and walked down the center aisle past the proud audience of friends and relatives. A gentle wind played in our mortar board tassels. The sun was high overhead and there was not a cloud in the azure sky. We could not deal with or grasp the idea that most of us would never see one another again; so we concentrated instead on the beauty of the day and enjoying our great moment of triumph.

## CHOOSING A COLLEGE:

Dad had been researching various schools of higher learning while also comparing tuition costs. He thought I ought to attend New Jersey State Teachers College; but fate had other thoughts on the subject. At an elegant party, Mom, Dad, and I were introduced to Henry Lee Moon, an attractive dark-brown-skinned man who was the Director of Public Relations for the National Association for the Advancement of Colored People (NAACP). My uncle, Walter White, was the Executive Director of the NAACP. Uncle Walter and Eleanor Roosevelt were instrumental in Marian Anderson's historic concert at Washington's Lincoln Memorial, after, because of her color, she had been rudely forbidden to sing at Constitution Hall.

Perhaps Henry Lee Moon had heard about me from my Uncle Walter or maybe an idea struck him out of the blue. The light friendly discourse took on a serious tone. Mr. Moon confided to us that Sarah Lawrence College, an elegant, progressive all girls college in Bronxville, New York was searching for just the right students "of color" to further integrate the school. He strongly suggested that I apply.

I requested an application form, which I filled out and sent in with the required picture. At the formal interview, I took along some of my prize-winning high school art work, praying that it would impress them. My heart leapt for joy when I received their letter of acceptance. I was then officially, thanks to Henry Lee Moon's intervention, a freshman at Sarah Lawrence College.

# College

## GETTING READY FOR COLLEGE:

In order to make a fashionable fall wardrobe for me to wear at Sarah Lawrence College, Mom set to work immediately buying material and patterns. She laid out the fabric on the dining room table and placed the individual patterns carefully on top. I loved listening in to her inner thoughts (she seemed to be speaking to herself). As she talked, she pointed to what was to become sleeves, a skirt, or perhaps a bodice. "Now --- this is this and that is that --- so if this is this and that's that --- what is this?" as she pointed incredulously to one piece of the pattern. "Now let me go through this one more time. If this is this and that's that --- then --- this is that!" Breaking out into a broad grin and clapping her hands together, she would then start to cut around the pattern she had just figured out.

I was the first in Mom's family to attend college. They all pitched in to help in any way they could. For example, Aunt Annie donated her fur coat to the cause. She called it a "mar-mink." (I am not sure what kind of animal that was). Aunt Virgie gave my father money to help with the astronomically expensive tuition.

After a blistering hot summer of getting my brand new woolen wardrobe ready, Mom lovingly folded and packed it into a steamer trunk to be sent to my new home in Bronxville, New York. With many hugs, kisses and well wishes from all, I was finally off to experience a new, different and thrilling life as a college freshman.

## SARAH LAWRENCE COLLEGE:

Sarah Lawrence was a student friendly school, so, at long last, I was in my element. My studies, to name a few, ranged from painting and sculpture to voice, physiology, sociology and

Spanish. There were no prerequisites for taking any course and no exams. The classes were very small (6 to 9 people) and, if it was a nice day outside, the class was convened on the great green lawn of the campus. The unique mission of the college was to provide individualized education of which each student takes ownership. Because of the small classes, there was no place for the student to hide. Therefore one always had to be prepared for class and the frequent one-on-one conferences with the professor.

Sarah Lawrence College girls were known for burning the midnight oil as they wrote, read, then wrote some more. At the end of a semester, we received a written report from the professor complimenting us on what we had achieved and making suggestions how we could further excel. There were no required grades, but reports could be transcribed into grades if requested.

My classmates included Barbara Walters (who later became a television legend), Beverly Pabst of Blue Ribbon Beer fame and Eve DuPont. In addition, such names as Guggenheim and Rothschild were commonplace. Even though Mom's hand crafted clothes were elegant and just right for special occasions, dungarees were the dress of the day.

I joined a singing group called the Double Quartet or "DQ's," which was the Sarah Lawrence answer to the Yale Whiffenpoofs. We sang at many college functions. One of our songs was written by a male student. Yes, Sarah Lawrence College was an all girls school at the time, but after World War II a few returning male veterans were admitted as students. The words to the song went like this: "And when I jump into beddie all ready for Eddie, I hope that Eddie will be ready for me." Needless to say we all worried about what our parents in the audience would think. We hoped they would not be too shocked.

The Music Department decided to put on a mini-staged production of George Gershwin's classic opera _Porgy and Bess_. I was the only person "of color" in the cast and sang the role of Bess. Porgy was sung by Connie Lerner, the daughter of Max Lerner, a well known newspaper columnist. The only men in the cast were the World War II veterans who added much veracity to the crap shooting scene. When the Chairman of the Music Department heard the performance, he was astounded that Betty Powell, a painting and sculpture student, could sing so well. He surprised me by offering me a full music scholarship, which pleased my parents.

## FAILURE AS A BUDDING NIGHT CLUB SINGER:
After my success in _Porgy and Bess_, a light bulb switched on in my mind when I realized that Barbara Walter's father was Lou Walters, the owner of The Latin Quarter, a famous night club in New York City. I said to myself, "What if I asked Barbara to inveigle an audition to sing for her father?" Barbara did as I asked. Before I knew it, she had spoken to him, securing both a date and time for me to be heard. Even though I was fully rehearsed, when the audition date finally arrived, cold shivers hit me and my heart began to beat faster and faster. I hid in my dorm room and stared at the clock as the hands neared and then went past the appointed time. I sheepishly apologized to Barbara, telling her that fear had prevented me from getting on the train to New York. Thank goodness her affection for me did not and has yet to falter. In fact many years after our graduation in 1951, Barbara and I played a major role at a Lincoln Center gala, celebrating the 50th Anniversary of the founding of Sarah Lawrence College.

After the Latin Quarter debacle, I realized that the stage fright monster still remained alive and well hidden in the dark recesses of my unseasoned performer's mind. As is often said, "Wisdom is the better part of valor." So, in retrospect, I believe I did the right thing by not singing for Lou Walters. I now know I was totally unprepared for the New York night club scene and that pursuing a career as a jazz singer would have disappointed my parents. After all, I was the possessor and guardian of a gloriously beautiful voice capable of singing the most difficult of music. It had been passed down genetically from my beloved grandfather, Poppy.

## DANCING WITH ARTHUR MURRAY:

During my college days, the Arthur Murray Dance Studios were nationally known for teaching an elegant style of ballroom dancing made famous by Arthur Murray himself. I was intrigued to meet and sing with his twin daughters, who also attended Sarah Lawrence College. They both enjoyed participating in the College's many musical activities, especially the Double Quartet. Through their efforts, arrangements were made for the "DQ's" to sing along with the Yale Whiffenpoofs on The Arthur Murray Show, a highly rated prime time television variety show.

Hours before show time, we were driven from Bronxville to a TV studio theater in New York City. As my eyes adjusted to the darkness I caught a glimpse of someone in the shadows. I said to myself, "I know who that is but ---- where's his fur and long tail?" Yes, it was Burt Lahr, the famed Cowardly Lion from the movie classic, The Wizard of Oz. Next to him was Burl Ives, a well known folk singer. They too, were appearing on the show that evening. I impatiently waited to be introduced to them, along with the other girls of the Quartet. The man doing the introductions was quite tall, slender and lithe, and wearing an impeccably tailored suit. It was none other than the famous Arthur Murray.

After the TV show, Mr. Murray invited us all to join him at the Copacabana to celebrate our success. Now the Copacabana (or "Copa," as it was commonly referred to) was an elite and "in" night club. When the jazz band returned from their break, the great Arthur Murray asked me to dance. Other patrons joined us on the small dance floor. Because the sensuous music began to throb in our blood and brains, we undulated a rhythmic, classic jitterbug. As the insistent beat continued on, we became more expansive in our movements, taking up more and more space on the postage stamp dance floor. I must say we were rather startled when one of the "Copa" employees came to warn us, "You can't dance that way here! There is little space left for our other patrons." It occurred to me then that this person did not know to whom he was speaking so critically. If he had, he most certainly would have bitten his tongue until it bled. After all, Arthur Murray was then considered to be the world's best known ballroom dancer!

## AN EARLY MARRIAGE:

The war veterans at Sarah Lawrence College were very pleased to be accepted into a "top of the mark" all girls school. There were many beautiful girls in youth's full flower, but very few bees to pollinate them. The veterans added greatly to the overall depth and breadth of class discussions. They had been out in the real world, while we had essentially led sheltered lives.

I was intrigued by one of the veterans in particular. On impulse at the age of 19, I married him. His mother came to the hotel to meet me while we were on our honeymoon. Hearing a knock on the door, I opened it to see a short older woman with fear in her eyes. She exclaimed looking at me, "Oy --- so tall! You know when you have children, they'll all be born with tails!"

I did enjoy our first summer together when we were both camp counselors in the Catskills, and I learned to play the guitar by ear and sang folk songs. However, after a brief period of time, while commuting daily to Sarah Lawrence from New York, I made an honest assessment of our lives together and weighed all the elements. I decided to permanently leave our 14th Street walk-up apartment. After a quick Florida divorce, I regained my freedom and returned to my former single life on campus.

## RETURN TO THE SARAH LAWRENCE CAMPUS:

I again felt liberated and enjoyed being back on campus. I moved into an off-campus facility with five other girls across from the College's main entrance which was bordered by two enormous wrought iron gates. The letters SLC were artistically placed near the top of each gate and easily discernible. From the gate, a road went up a small hill to the administration building called "Westlands." This edifice was formerly a Tudor style private mansion with many peaks and chimneys.

## MEETING DOUG JONES FOR THE FIRST TIME:

One day my classmate and friend Madelon asked me for a big favor. She wanted me to go, at the appropriate time, to the reception desk at "Westlands" to intercept a young man who was coming up from New York to see her. She said, "Tell him I'm very sorry I can't see him today and to please forgive me. I've got to go see a close relative who has just been rushed to the hospital." I asked, "What's his name?" She replied, "Doug Jones. He's studying engineering and absolutely loves opera."

Looking at my watch, I thought I had better get going since it was almost time for him to arrive. With the speed of a greyhound, I hustled up to the Westlands reception desk to welcome him, but he had already arrived. I called his name and extended my hand. His warm brown hand enveloped mine as he greeted me with a baritone voice of incomparable beauty. His athletic looking, well muscled body was at least 6'-3" and his brown hewed Paul Robesonesque facial features matched his voice. After I delivered Madelon's message of regret (mission accomplished), we stood and chatted for a short while. He seemed to have a warm calm and quiet inner core. I was totally enchanted by his presence and wanted to know more about this opera loving engineering student.

At the first opportunity, I corralled Madelon and plied her with many questions. I was relieved when she said she did not consider Doug to be one of her current boyfriends and that she had known him and his family since childhood. I then asked, "Tell me, does he get along with his mother? My ex-husband couldn't stand his." She answered, "Oh yes, he's a very nice young man and good to his mother." She then surprised me by volunteering, "I've heard through the grapevine that he possesses a non-prehensile appendage that measures nearly a foot long when unfurled." A giggle gathered in the pit of my stomach. Just like an air bubble in the bathtub, it made its way to the surface. I resisted the temptation to guffaw. Feigning innocence, I shyly nodded approval instead.

**The girls at Sarah Lawrence College (1948 Collier's Magazine Article)**
**I'm 2nd from right**

## GRADUATION FROM SARAH LAWRENCE AND SEEING DOUG AGAIN:

The long anticipated graduation from Sarah Lawrence College in 1951 finally arrived for me and my classmates. It was held on the great lawn in front of Westlands and the weather was perfect. Doug Jones, who I last saw in the Westlands living room, was one of Madelon's graduation guests. At the end of the formal ceremony, he came over to offer me his congratulations and asked if he could take my picture. My dear old Aunt Virgie was standing next to me and surreptitiously whispered in my ear, "Who's he? He seems really nice!" Mom, Dad and my other relatives who were present all smiled broadly in agreement.

Stars, palms or tea leaves? If I could have read the future, I would have seen that this budding attraction would soon develop quintessentially into a very meaningful and long lasting relationship with music as its sustaining chord. Doug would eventually become my biggest promoter and my blessed "L'homme aux Chocolat" (My Chocolate Man).

# Remarried and on to The Suburbs

**FIRST JOBS:**
After graduation from Sarah Lawrence College with a
Bachelor of Arts Degree, I managed to find emotionally
unrewarding work in a shoe factory and then as a sales person
at Jay Thorpe, an elite women's high fashion store on 57th
Street in Manhattan. I then became an assistant first grade
teacher at Fieldston, a private progressive school in Riverdale.
My most fulfilling job by far, however, was working with
children at a Day Care Center on 116th Street. I finally had
the opportunity to use my talent at telling intriguing tales and
singing folk songs. Children were my first real audience, and
this experience was to be of great value to me in the future.
If one can hold the attention of little tots, one can hold
everybody's.

**RENEWING MY CONTACT WITH DOUG AND
FIRST DATE:**
I kept in touch with Madelon throughout the readjustment
period of my life. She was instrumental in finding me a nice
place to live in a beautiful brownstone on 145th Street just off
Riverside Drive. Madelon lived with her family in a
brownstone next door. I popped over to visit her one warm
Saturday afternoon. Still being curious about Doug Jones, I
asked about him. She answered my question with another
question. "Do you want his telephone number?" "Yes!" I
said with growing excitement. I immediately used her phone
and dialed the number she had given me. Madelon only
heard half the conversation, "Hello" --- "May I speak to
Doug Jones" --- "Oh you're his mother?" --- "He's not in?" ---
"Please tell him that Betty Powell, who he met at Sarah
Lawrence College, called. I have just moved and can't
remember my new phone number, so could he please call
Madelon Delany back instead." I tactfully deflected her next
question, "What do you want with him?," silently answering

to myself. "Wouldn't you like to know." Then I thanked her warmly and said goodbye.

As soon as I got home, I called Madelon to give her my new number. Later that afternoon, the telephone rang and I heard my name called loudly, "Betty, Betty it's for you!" Yes, it was the telephone call for which I was impatiently waiting. Right then and there, Doug asked me for a date. He said, "Tomorrow evening, an all George Gershwin Concert will be performed outdoors at Lewisohn Stadium by the New York Philharmonic Orchestra with Oscar Levant as featured soloist. Would you like to go with me?" I gleefully accepted! This was to be the first of many pleasurable musical experiences we would enjoy together. At dinner in a restaurant before the concert, he shared with me his thoughts about current Broadway productions and his all-consuming love of opera. It seemed that he attended his first opera performance at the age of eight. It was Wagner's _Lohengrin_ at the Metropolitan Opera House. He had been enchanted by it ever since. In college, he sang in the glee club, the chapel choir and, after graduation, in the New York Oratorio Society. He also appeared in college theatrical productions and later on in Off-Broadway shows while holding down a full time engineering job by day.

As the musicians took their places at the stadium concert, the lights brightened on stage. The stars and moon beautified a navy colored velvet sky as a plane flew overhead with blinking lights added to the excitement of the evening. Doug leaned over and whispered to me, just before applause welcomed the entrance of the conductor, "You know I knew about you back when we were teenagers. I always wanted to meet you." He then took my hand and held it throughout the concert.

## SOLIDIFYING MY RELATIONSHIP WITH DOUG:

As time passed, our relationship continued to warm and deepen, becoming more and more passionate. As luck would have it, Doug's mother, who had been widowed for many years, decided to re-marry and move out of their apartment. Several months after her wedding, at Doug's request, I packed up my things and moved in with him.

I soon found out, when I went to visit my parents in Plainfield, that they were less than pleased with my living without benefit of clergy. Dad surprised me late one evening as he padded down the hall in his nightclothes from their bedroom, the room where I was born. I had been trying unsuccessfully to fall asleep when I became aware of his presence in my bedroom. He said, "Your mother and I have been discussing you and Doug. She said that I should share with you what we think. Our conclusion is that you should either SHIT OR GET OFF THE POT! Doug's too nice a guy." Turning on his heels he nervously retraced his steps back to their bedroom. There were a few moments of near silence while Dad quietly recounted to Mom what he had just told me. Then Mom's voice painfully screamed out, "Oh no, Bill! --- you didn't say that to her! I thought we had decided on something else. Bill, how could you!"

After that episode, I did a lot of soul-searching and came to the conclusion that I desperately needed to have a heart-to-heart talk with Doug. One evening after some steamy love making, I propped myself up on my elbows and said decisively, " I've felt for quite a while as though we've been stealing from the altar. I truly think we ought to get married." He kissed me and replied with an impish grin, "I think so, too!"

## WEDDING AND HONEYMOON:

As soon as Mom heard that our wedding date had been set, she was relieved and immediately started searching for material and a pattern for my wedding dress. Since I had been married before, we did not think a white dress was appropriate. Together we chose an off-white champagne colored fabric. She and Aunt Virgie worked together on the wedding gown and honeymoon wardrobe. They were completed in time for our special "I do" day.

**Honeymoon on "Queen of Bermuda" (1954)**

After the wedding, we celebrated our new status by spending the first week of our honeymoon sightseeing in New York City. Among other things, we found the view from the top of the Empire State Building inspiringly awesome and felt a warm surge of patriotism when visiting the Statue of Liberty. At the end of the week, we boarded a cruise ship, the *Queen of Bermuda*, heading for its namesake. I had no inkling as to what a serious boating enthusiast I had just married. One would have thought he was the captain. He absolutely had to be on deck, even if it was at 4:00 in the morning, looking over the rail every time the ship either weighed anchor or docked.

## BERMUDA:
One sunny morning, bright and early, the *Queen of Bermuda* jockeyed herself gingerly into position to dock at a pier along Front Street in Hamilton, Bermuda. The phantom captain

Doug was on deck making sure it was all done correctly. We suffered pangs of nostalgia leaving our temporary home. This particular ship had exquisitely titillated all our senses and fulfilled every deep longing wish. We bid farewell to the captain and crew in their starched white uniforms. A native band then piped us down the gangplank to waiting taxicabs and cars lined up on the pier. One particular car separated itself from the others and pulled up close to us. The driver leaned out calling, "Are you Mr. and Mrs. Jones? I'm here to take you to Sunset Lodge". We nodded and got into the car. The driver then introduced himself as the owner of Sunset Lodge and in no time, we arrived at our destination.

**On our honeymoon in Bermuda (1954)**

Sunset Lodge was a large pink concrete building, with an electric blue tile roof, overlooking the ocean. On our first night, we heard the percussive harmonies of a steel drum band wafting through the open windows and under the door of our room. Curious, we followed the sound, and discovered its source. It came from an open air patio connected to the Lodge. Under dim lights, we saw a calypso band and a dance floor with many people whose hips fluidly swung to the rhythms of the island music. Black people danced only with black people and white people only with white people. When the musical set was over and the band took their break, the black people returned to tables on one side of the dance floor and the whites to the other. There was no intermingling at the tables either, so we sat with our black brothers and sisters, with whom we felt comfortable. Our "color" also dictated that we were not welcome anywhere but at a black owned hotel. The shock of this realization began to dim when a black entertainer called "The Leopard Man" jumped upon the bandstand dressed only in a leopard skin. In the middle of his act he asked the audience, "Are there any newlyweds here tonight? If so please rise!" We stood up along with the other honeymooners present. He continued, "Can you tell us please," he said with a lilting West Indian accent, "Is there anything that you have found out about your new mate that you didn't know before you married?" I raised my hand above my head and he nodded in my direction. I replied with a smothered laugh, "He sings in his sleep!" The Leopard Man paused then countered with, "What does he sing --- I need thee every hour?" In my mind's ear, I will always hear the surprised titter and the appreciative applause that followed.

## STARTING A FAMILY:

Back home in our New York apartment four months later on New Year's Day, I felt the need to have another little tete-a-tete with my "Mr. Jones". "Doug," I said running my hand over his very wavy hair, "You know --- you're 29 and I'm 24 years old. I think it's about time we started our family." Just then the telephone rang. Doug sprang up to answer it. I heard, "Oh, hi Mom! --- Happy New Year to you too! --- What's my New Year's resolution? We're going to have a family!" Polite friendly chatter continued for a few more sentences. After saying goodbye to his mother, Doug hung up the phone, took my hand and led me into the bedroom.

## MOVING TO CONNECTICUT:

Then pregnant, I could not find any merit in trying to raise a family in a walk-up New York apartment in a tough, tough neighborhood, so we decided to find somewhere else to live. First we checked out homes in New Jersey where we both had grown up, but most of the ones we saw just did not please us. Doug daily searched the real estate sections of the newspapers. One day, he brought an advertisement for me to read. I could tell by his demeanor that he had found a house which intrigued him. "Sweetie Pie," he cooed, "I really think we ought to drive up and see this one. It sounds like it's just what we've been looking for; a ranch house (all on one floor) with a large living room, three bedrooms, three bathrooms, all set on a two acre parcel in Wilton, Connecticut." We immediately jumped into our car and sped up the Merritt Parkway. On the ride up, I remembered my father's advice to us when buying a house. "Make sure the outside of the house is stone and the inside is wood paneled so you won't have to paint. Make sure it's set on enough land so you can't hear your next door neighbor flush the toilet and that the house is all on one floor so you can grow old in it."

**Our Wilton, CT. House (1955)**

As we entered the driveway, I saw before me a grey fieldstone ranch house set almost 200 feet from the road. We were welcomed by the owner into a spacious living room with a high vaulted ceiling, a brick fireplace, tan wood paneling and no stairs to climb. In Dad's last days, he came to live with us and was able to navigate the entire house with his walker. He marveled at the view of the grass, gurgling stream and pine trees from the window of the large combination music room, dining room and art studio. He sighed, "How beautiful!" I complimented him with, "Well Dad, --- you ordered it."

The owner seemed to like us very much, so after much discussion, he and Doug agreed on a price of $18,500. However, he wanted some money down to hold it for us. Doug pulled out his wallet and showed him all the money he had with him at the time, a $20 and a $5 dollar bill. The owner then said reassuringly, "That will do it. You seem to be a nice young couple. I'm Jewish, so I particularly want to sell to you people. Maybe Wilton will learn something by so doing."

We moved in but unintentionally brought along some six-legged transplants from New York. Stowaway roaches scurried out of our boxes to find a safe haven in the kitchen cabinets. I found one of their kin blithely riding the minute hand of the kitchen clock. I then heard a strange sound coming down the hall from the spare bedroom where the partially emptied barrels and boxes were temporarily stored. "Tap, tap, tap" ---- then something being dragged. Over and over the sounds repeated, coming nearer and nearer. Increasing curiosity demanded that I look down the hall to see what it was. Much to my surprise, I saw a little grey mouse that had finally freed itself from under some personal objects in one of the barrels, the weight of which had damaged one of its legs. My grandfather "Poppy," in a similar situation, when a trap had caught only the mouse's tail and caused it to run in circles with the trap clattering behind it, raised his foot and quickly stomped on the mouse, sending it to "mouse heaven" forever.  Having been present at that execution,  I said to myself, "it's either you or me, mouse!" and did the same thing Poppy had done ---- Stomp  and squish!

## FIRST BORN:

As the delivery date of our first born neared, I became more and more apprehensive about facing labor in our new home in the wilds of Wilton and without a family member nearby. We decided that it might relieve some of my anxieties to drive into New York and spend the waiting time under the warm, watchful eye of Doug's encouraging Mother, Chris.

When we arrived, Chris had already made up for us the folding double bed in her living room. Doug and I dined alone that evening in a nearby restaurant.  I began to feel poorly and lost my appetite.  We walked back to the apartment, and I went straight to bed.

In the middle of the night, I went into labor. I woke Doug, who in turn awakened his Mother.  After timing my contractions, she said to him, "Go put your clothes on, dear, and take her to the hospital."  I got up, put my clothes on, and lumbered into the bathroom.  I felt like one of the tomato worms in Dad's garden. I used to delight in stepping on them.  If I did it just right, the worm exploded in two directions at once.

Feeling better, I returned from the bathroom to find Doug completely dressed but, ---- why he was back in bed?  As I drew closer, It dawned on me that this whole event had proven to be emotionally much too much for him.  He had fainted dead away, fully clothed.

After this momentary setback, Doug got the car and drove me safely to the hospital.  He then waited anxiously in a special room for several hours with the other expectant fathers.  I must have been a fertile turtle because nine months to the day on October 2, 1955, the nurses on duty were dumbfounded by the high decibel cry of our new born son, Jeffrey. He already had all the equipment to become a singer if he so desired. Although he had just been born, the potentials were already astoundingly audible. When the doctor finally told Doug he was now a new father, he ran down the hospital hall to find me. Bursting into my room, he rushed toward the bed. Lovingly, he grabbed me up in his arms, whispering passionately, with tears in his eyes, "Thank you, Sweetie Pie." He later told me that the next instant he thought to himself, "But why is a strange man sitting next to Betty's bed?" Alarmed by this realization, he looked more closely at what he believed was me and was rocked to his inner core to discover the woman he had just grabbed was not me at all. He had gone into the wrong room and swept a complete stranger into his arms, thanking her for having his baby, while her husband looked on in stunned amazement.

## LIVING IN WILTON:

We were one of the first African-American families to live in Wilton. Most of the people we met were warm and accepting, but when Doug went to the local market for the first time, he was politely asked at the check-out counter, "Who are you working for?" Doug replied, "I don't work for anybody. I've just moved to Wilton." The clerk nervously smiled and nodded saying, "Oh, I see."

After settling down, we both joined the Wilton Congregational Church and sang in the Choir. I sang alto for many years, never knowing that I was really a soprano, and Doug was in the bass section. The Church came to our rescue when the barber in Wilton Center refused to cut our son's hair. Doug asked him "You won't cut his hair or you don't know how to cut his hair?" The barber said in Italian accented English, "I won't-a cut-a his hair." I told our Minister what had happened. Unknown to me he reported this incident to the Connecticut Civil Rights Commission and they sent a representative to investigate. Through the grapevine, word got back to us that the barber answered the investigator's questions in consternation, "I'm-a-so-sorry! I thought-a that if-a-people saw a black kid in-a-chair through the window, they wouldn't come to me anymore. You tell-a-his Momma to bring-a-him in! -- Sure, I'll cut-a-his hair." I took Jeff to the barber just once to prove a point, then bought a pair of dog clippers and did the work myself from then on.

## WILTON PLAYSHOP:

Elizabeth, a soprano stood not far from me in the Wilton Congregational Church Choir. Her husband Jim Barnum, who was genetically linked to P.T. Barnum of circus fame, also sang in the choir. Jim had previously heard me play the guitar and sing folk songs, but after I sang a dramatic solo in Church one Sunday morning, he approached me after the service, "That was very good!" Then he said, "I'm currently involved with a new production at the Wilton Playshop. We're going to celebrate the opening of our newly refurbished theater by performing an opera. It will be Gian-Carlo Menotti's *The Medium,* and as a curtain raiser we will do Mozart's *Bastien and Bastienne*. With your permission, I'd like to suggest you for the lead role of Madame Flora in *The Medium.* After hearing you sing that solo in church this morning, I really think you are just right for the role."

The vocal category of Madame Flora is that of a mezzo soprano, one of the lower female voice ranges. Because I had sung alto for so many years, I had no trouble with the low notes but problems did occur with the higher ones. My friend Elizabeth Barnum, a high soprano, helped me, technically, with those. During *Medium* rehearsals, the director seemed to be fully satisfied with the positive results of Elizabeth's special coaching.

We were to be accompanied by two pianos. Since I was having so much trouble with Menotti's difficult score, one of the accompanists spent many hours teaching me the music note by note. To this day, I thank my lucky stars we moved to Wilton because this is where I was given the opportunity to grow both musically and theatrically. I quickly learned among, other things, the meaning of various director's terminology, specifically upstage right, upstage left, downstage left, center stage, et cetera

Unfortunately, the Playshop kept putting off the opening date of _The Medium_ due to the construction of a new backstage addition to the theater. I was already pregnant with our second child and with each postponement, I kept growing bigger and bigger. After much thought on this ticklish matter, I was finally able to solve the problem. I said to myself, "My breasts will have to stick out further than my ever expanding waist." So I balled up several lengths of material and stuffed them into the breast of my costume. Voila! --- It worked just as I had thought. The role of Madame Flora is that of a large overpowering woman, and with all the extra padding, my waistline actually looked more slender.

Madame Flora, the charlatan, eked out an existence as a psychic medium. Clients came to her dingy apartment, where she conducted seances, assisted by her daughter Monica and a mute Gypsy youth named Toby. As the lights dimmed, Monica stood behind a white curtain and her voice added veracity to the seance. The clients believed it was coming from their beloved departed, while Toby pulled levers to make the table rise and fall and also provided other sound effects during the ritual.

In one scene, during a seance, Madame Flora, acting as though she was in a complete trance, felt a hand touch her neck. She knew she was a liar and a fake and could not really contact the spirits of the dead. Madame Flora suspected Toby of touching her and was determined to make him confess. After the clients left, she whipped Toby unmercifully to make him own up and say that it was indeed he who had touched her. I was given a five foot long woven leather whip to do the job on stage. I knew beyond the shadow of a doubt that, as Madame Flora's character took command of my mind, voice, and body in the performance, I could mistakenly inflict pain and injury with this particular kind of whip. For the sake of the actor playing the role of Toby, I asked for something else to do the task. I was then given a stick covered in wool with three long lengths of wool. During the actual performance, I was so carried away that I actually broke the stick on his back. He shot me a disbelieving glance as he slipped to the floor. During the cast party after opening night, he carefully gave me a wide swath, purposely never coming within arm's reach.

There are some singers who swear never to sing the role of Madame Flora, because the slow disintegration of her personality threatens the underpinning of their own sanity. As an example, during the second act Madame Flora began to hear disembodied voices herself which were not Monica's. She immediately canceled all the seances, thereby disappointing her faithful clientele. The fear and distress she felt caused her to begin drinking. With a bottle of wine beside her on the table, Madame Flora sang about the terrible life she had led. She drank more and more. At this point in the performance, my mother who was in the audience, white knuckled my father's arm and said to him in a stage whisper, "Oh Billy ---- I taught her never to drink like that ---- I'm so embarrassed." I guess Mom lost contact with reality, too, and forgot that I was only acting.

At this point in the opera, Madame Flora slobbery drunk, knocked her bottle off the table. From my vantage point on the stage, I could see the audience's reaction when the bottle loudly crashed to the floor. En masse, they seemed to levitate from their chairs in fear. Madame Flora's eyes closed temporarily from so much drinking, thereby signaling Toby to come out of hiding and slip behind the white curtain used during seances. Madame Flora awakened suddenly and saw the curtain flutter. She opened the table drawer, took out her pistol and taking aim -- shot at the curtain. The audience saw a small red spot appear. It morphed into a slowly descending rivulet of blood running down the curtain. We saw Toby's two hands grab both sides of the curtain. He then pitched forward tearing it down as he fell to the floor, covered in blood. Madame Flora menacingly stood over the body asking slowly, "Was it you? ---- Was it you?"

At the opera's end, the stage curtains slowly closed and the audience members were finally able to loosen the tight grip they had on the arms of their chairs and relax. A majority jumped to their feet yelling "Bravo! --- Bravo!" at the top of their lungs and clapped and clapped until their arms must have grown tired.

**Our Wilton, CT. House after complete renovation (1965)**

# In Africa

By the time the show at the Wilton Playshop was over, I had grown much too big in the middle to fit into my regular clothes. Winter was fast approaching. Mom's phone rang just as she had bitten the last thread off the expandable waisted woolen maternity clothes she had made for me. She rushed expectantly and picked up the receiver. "Hi Mom," I breathlessly whispered. "Darling," she chirped brightly, "How are things?" "Oh Mom," I exclaimed, "I just got off the phone with Doug. It seems he's been offered a big job heading a large engineering project in Liberia, West Africa. He's to supervise the construction of a 150 mile road and also a new water filtration plant for the capital city of Monrovia. We've got to fly there as soon as possible"

I thought Mom was changing the subject when she said, "I went to a tea leaf reader today. She told me that some close member of my family would be going to Africa. For the life of me, I couldn't figure out what she was talking about but now, I see she was right on the beam. Come down to Plainfield dear," she continued, "and we'll go find some light-weight cotton material for maternity clothes, to keep you cool in Africa." Among the material I finally chose was a "chickens sitting on eggs" design because in essence that was exactly what I was doing, sitting on my egg.

Our young son Jeff, Doug and I took off via Pan American Airways from New York's Idlewild Airport (later renamed JFK) for the 30 hour flight to Monrovia, Liberia with intermediate stops in Boston, the Azores, Lisbon and Dakar. The flight was lengthy because the year was 1956, prior to the jet age. Despite all my interest in Africa, being pregnant with our second child dampened the joyful buoyancy of my psyche. I had always longed to experience living in a country where the black man ruled. Now at long last it seemed I was going to get the chance.

During the long flight, I had the opportunity to read about the history of Liberia. In 1822 it was first colonized by 88 freed American Negro slaves. This venture was made possible by the American Colonization Society. Their purpose was "to promote and execute a plan for colonization in Africa of free people of color, with their consent, residing in the United States of America." Some people felt it a serious threat to allow freed black men, particularly the free mulatto, to continue to reside next to slaves at a time when rebellion was a distinct possibility. Others were moved to action by the most altruistic and humanitarian reasons. Freed Negro slaves were happy to leave the United States to escape inequality and prejudice here; yet, once in Liberia, they too were accused by the whole world of actually indulging in slave trade themselves.

Upon landing at Robertsfield in Monrovia, named after the United States President James Monroe, we were picked up at the airport by someone from Doug's new office. What a change from Connecticut's snow and ice to Liberia's hot humid climate, similar to a Turkish bath. It almost proved too much for poor pregnant me. I could not wait to shed my winter maternity suit and don my cotton "chickens sitting on eggs" outfit.

After going through Liberian customs and getting all our luggage packed into the car, we started the long drive to Monrovia. As the sun slid towards its rendezvous with the horizon, I watched, entranced, as this new world whizzed by. We drove through mile after mile of tapped rubber trees, leased by Firestone, adjacent to beautiful mahogany forests. Our driver told us that besides rubber and mahogany, Liberia had many other natural resources, including iron ore considered to be the purist in the world, and diamonds found in stream beds. From my open car window, I could see native fires light up villages, silhouetting stately trees and human forms as we passed by.    Finally, after what seemed to be hours, we came to a stop in front of an iron gate attached to an eight foot tall stone wall surrounding our new domicile. The driver tooted his horn to alert the houseboys within to come out and unlock the gate.

Hearing the car horn, a houseboy came out of the house, his footsteps quickening with excited anticipation.    After polite introductions, we followed him up onto the porch and into a fully furnished house the company had leased for us.    They had also engaged a household staff of seven to take care of our every need.    The spacious living room, with its maroon marble floor, was furnished with bent wood bamboo chairs and comfortable cushions.    We were to eat all our meals at a matching dining room table.    Next to the dining room was a fully equipped kitchen, and down the hall were three bedrooms.

It was not until the next morning that we met all seven of the household help and I had the opportunity to see, in the bright sunlight, the outside of this attractive red and white concrete house, with its tan shutters and a tile roof.    There was not a blade of grass allowed to grow within the confines of the walled area because snakes might slither in and hide unseen in the undergrowth.    If the green or black mamba snake bites someone, he is dead in three to five minutes.    One of the houseboys was assigned to keeping the area within the walls completely bare of brush.    Another was given the task of taking care of our recently acquired dog.    His mother was named "Two Cents," so we named him "Half Penny."    If we had allowed the dog free range outside of the walled area, he would have been quickly snatched up, cooked, and eaten. Protein was a very scarce and precious commodity.

## LIBERIAN GOVERNMENT:

Liberia, under the benevolent dictatorship of Dr. William V.S. Tubman, was politically,  a one party system.    In order to vote, one had to be at least 21 years old and a person of color. No white person or white run business could own land; they could only lease it. The average wage at the time was approximately 80 cents per day. There was no middle class to speak of. A citizen either walked barefoot in rags or rode in air-conditioned cars.

At most social functions, pomp and circumstance reigned. White tie, tails and top hat were the order of the day. Since Doug was the head of a major U.S. company, we were automatically included in President Tubman's invitation list, enabling us to attend formal gatherings at the Executive Mansion (Liberia's White House). At these affairs, the ladies were all beautifully gowned in a native cloth called "a lapa". The Frontier Force Marching Band provided pulsating brass and drum music. In no time at all, we learned to dance their national dance called the "Quadrille". It looked like a hip swinging version of the "Virginia Reel" and was done to a swaying "African-Calypso" beat. The dance was brought to Liberia on the first boats from America by the freed slaves and is still intact.

As the evening grew late, and if President Tubman was having a particularly good time, he gave orders to lock all the doors and post guards to see that no one left. We soon learned from others to anticipate this turn of events and to slip out before being locked in. The President, however, would always serve breakfast to his guests when parties continued beyond sun-up.

## PRINCE BERNHARD'S VISIT:
Prince Bernhard of Holland planned a visit to see President Tubman. In preparation, a month before his arrival there was a beehive of activity, including a massive clean-up of the area where the Prince would be visiting and the planting of trees lining the road from the airport to the Executive Mansion. Since the Prince would be flying his own plane and landing at the small Monrovia Airport, the gravel runway was quickly paved and potted flowering plants were placed along the

route he was to travel by car. The DC-3, with the Prince at the controls, flew over the horizon and came into view as it prepared to touch down. When the landing gear came into contact with the newly paved runway, the still soft surface adhered to the wheels, coating them more and more, until the plane ground to a complete and sudden stop. Behind it on the runway were two tire sized tracks of exposed bare earth. The embarrassment of President Tubman and his entire welcoming party, as they stood in their formal attire waiting to greet the Prince, was painfully evident.

## THE OTHER SIDE OF LIBERIA:
Even though we were lucky enough to live rather luxuriously, there were large numbers of extremely poor people living in the capital city of Monrovia. Trespassing and thievery were a common occurrence. If one wanted to protect his personal effects, his home had to be like a fortress, with decorative iron securing every window and a night watchman patrolling the grounds each and every night. Even though we had the required night watchman, many months after moving in a thief still managed to scale the wall and steal things undetected. As the sun rose the next morning, we found that while we slept, Doug's pants had been fished with a stick off the bedroom chair from where he had laid them the night before, and his wallet was missing. We searched the yard and finally found the wallet and pictures, but no money. I believe pictures from the past are more precious than money anyway, so I was overjoyed to repossess them intact.

## THE BIRTH OF OUR SECOND CHILD:
With my due date approaching, the child within my womb began giving me many an ever increasingly strong "let me outta here " kick! Doug and I felt a pressing need to visit the hospital in Monrovia, where I was to give birth. We were shocked to see most of the screens on the windows ripped and flapping in the breeze. Liberia was considered to have a high number of malaria cases. Proper screening should have been a top priority to stop this disease, so widely spread by

mosquitoes. In addition, there were rumors that babies had been eaten alive by rodents. I certainly did not fly all this distance to have my newborn child made into baby sushi by hungry rats! We therefore made an immediate decision not to use this unsafe facility.

What should we do? Go back to the United States, or perhaps Europe, where many ex-patriots went to have their babies? Doug's Chief Engineer, Leonard Abrams, told us about an excellent American Doctor, who was in charge of the Lutheran Mission Hospital in Zorzor, an hour's plane ride from Monrovia. Since Doug's company had an office in Zorzor, where Abrams was based, arrangements were made for the doctor, Earl Reber, to fly down to Monrovia to examine me. As he bent over to peer into my darker depths, I suddenly heard a strange sound. ---- Dr Reber's pants had ripped open right up the back. I tried to muffle a reactive giggle as best I could but alas, I failed.

Doug's company plane (a small 4-seat Piper) was requisitioned to fly me to the Hospital in Zorzor. The co-pilot's wheel was removed to make room for me and my child within. Weighing over 200 pounds, I could not imagine how we would ever manage to take off. Revving the engine faster and faster, to counteract the extra weight, the plane finally became airborne. Once aloft, pilot Major Dunne gave me a first rate tour as we flew over mile after mile of tangled wilderness, small native villages, muddy rivers and burning, smoldering patches of land. We could actually smell the smoke as it rose high into the atmosphere. Native farmers habitually cleared the land by burning it off, then planted rice, harvested it, and sold most of it, barely keeping enough for themselves to eat. They did not fertilize the land to regenerate the soil but simply burned off the underbrush on some other spot to be cultivated.

Zorzor was finally in sight. There was no airport, so the pilot had to watch carefully for cars and trucks on the road below, because that was where we were going to land. He slowed the engine and we lost altitude. Making sure it was all clear for landing, he touched down on the road, taxied a short distance to a clearing, then cut the engine altogether.

When the cockpit door was opened, I saw approximately 50 people lining the road and cheering when they caught a glimpse of me as I prepared to deplane. I was so heavy that I had to struggle in order to rise out of my seat and descend to the ground. As I inched slowly forward towards the open cockpit door, my skirt rose higher and higher like an ascending window shade, partially exposing me for all to see. Realizing my embarrassing predicament, everyone of the native welcoming party turned their backs in unison, to afford me the privacy I desperately desired.

Just as I stepped to the ground, I was greeted by two warm, smiling people, Lenny Abrams and his wife Ethel. At first glance, she looked very much like my Mother, quite short and a little overweight. I gave in to my first impulse by giving her a kiss and a daughterly hug. Lenny said, "We would like to take you to our house until it's time for you to go to the hospital." When we finally reached their home, I was tired, so they pulled out a cot and made up a bed for me. I sighed with joy, realizing that I could finally ".... lay my burden down ...." as the Negro spiritual goes. I sat down on the comfortable cot and stretched out. Lenny and Ethel started to leave the room but turned on their heels when they heard me let out a muffled yelp! They were stunned speechless when they saw what had happened. The bed had suddenly folded up --- with me in it! Thank goodness I was rescued, forthwith, and the two ends of the cot put back down on the floor. After checking myself out, I calmed their fears by assuring them that I was "just fine."

The next morning bright and early, I went into labor and was immediately taken to Zorzor's Lutheran Mission Hospital. The facility had no kitchen, so family members of patients had to cook for them on the floor next to their hospital beds. John, our cook from Monrovia, was driven up to prepare my meals. Originally he was supposed to fly to Zorzor with me but was much too frightened. He had never flown in a plane before. I was shown to my room and given a gown. Doctor Reber came in, examined me and said, "it's time to take her to the delivery room." While donning his surgical gown, he told me: "A spinal is the only anesthesia we can give you. We just don't have the up-to-date medical facilities for anything else."

In no time at all, everyone heard on June 22, 1957 the first cry of our new baby daughter, Janet. At that same instant, I splattered the doctor with red blood and said silently to myself: "A toast to you Doc! Here's blood in your eye! You sure know your business." Doctor Reber held Janet up by her feet and exclaimed, "Why she's half grown already!" I could see that she was well filled out by the shape of her round adorable buns. Reber confided, "You know there's such malnutrition here in Liberia that native newborns are usually half her size." Since the only electrical generator in Zorzor was at the hospital, in order to announce a successful birth to the entire town and so that everyone could join in the rejoicing, the lights were dimmed for an instant, once for a boy and twice for a girl.

The next day, John came to see me and exclaimed, "Thank you, Missy, for giving the world a new life." I was deeply touched. I could see he was carrying under his arm something with feathers. He presented it to me as a gift. It was a live, "clucking" chicken. He then tied it to the leg of my hospital bed. When I breast fed Janet, she would suck! suck! suck! By this time the chicken was hungry and protested with a cluck! cluck! cluck! Major Dunne, the pilot, also came to congratulate me. It seemed he had already heard about John's gift so, when he saw the chicken, he reached into his pocket and pulled out some grain. Chiding me, he commented as he scattered food on the floor, "Well the least you could do is feed it." That night, John cooked his gift for my dinner. Boy, it was one tough bird!

When I had sufficiently recovered from the birthing process and no longer needed to be in the hospital, Baby Janet and I were allowed to stay in a small concrete house which was owned by the Lutheran Mission. Since it was vacant at the time, we were able to stay there until Doug's arrival by company plane to take us home to Monrovia. A hand constructed utilitarian, solid mahogany crib with mosquito repelling screens on five sides was provided for Janet's comfort and safety. Lenny Abrams dropped us off and said, "I'll come right back with a bottle of clean drinking water." In Zorzor, one never drank the tap water. It could give one amoebic dysentery. In fact, one could not even let a drop of water enter one's mouth when taking a shower. It was much safer to take a bath in a tub.

Night began to descend as Lenny left. I made Janet as comfortable as possible. Because there were no window shades or curtains, I turned off the lights and took off my clothes. Before I was able to put on my night clothes, I saw the headlights of Lenny's car returning. When he reached the screen door on foot, he called out, "Why are all the lights off?" I yelled back, "I was getting ready for bed and was afraid I could be seen. There are no shades or blinds. Come to the screened porch door and just hand me the water around the corner of the door." So that Lenny would not see me naked, I pressed my body flat against the wall next to the door and extended my arm full length around it. In this position, I became aware of a strange sensation. The one breast that was pressed against the toggle switch began to tingle. The feeling ran down the entire length of my body to my feet. Lenny handed me the bottle which I grasped, and he left. I tried to push myself away from the wall but found that my breast was glued to the wall. So were my feet to the floor. It dawned on me that this feeling could be electricity coursing through my body due to faulty wiring in an ungrounded concrete building. My fear grew as I contemplated the possibility that, "I could be electrocuted!"

I gathered every ounce of my strength and pushed away from the wall, finally freeing myself from the immobilizing current. Afterwards, it occurred to me that when nursing Janet, my breast milk might temporarily take on a different taste because of this electrically charged episode. To deal with such an eventuality, luckily my father had made up and taught me a song many years ago. It was called the "Sour Milk Song." The words went: "Bum Titty, - Bum Titty, - Bum Titty, - Bum!"

After a short recovery period, Janet and I boarded the same plane for our return flight to Monrovia. It gave me the greatest pleasure to, at last, introduce our son Jeff to his new sister. They bonded immediately. I, of course, was just happy to be home and reunited with my family.

Mary, a new member of our household staff, was hired as a Nanny to perform the many menial tasks associated with the care of an infant. We always insisted that any prospective employee be examined by a doctor prior to being engaged. She passed the test. We did not hire one hopeful houseboy because, after the exam, he was diagnosed as having a dangerously life threatening communicable disease. One cannot be too careful, you know!

Janet grew like a rose planted in black soil and watered by nightly rain. Very soon, she and Jeff could play together indoors, during the six month rainy season, on their solid mahogany double slide we had built for them. When sunshine finally ended that season, they particularly enjoyed playing outdoors and carrying their teddy bears on their backs as the native women carried their babies.

## LIFE IN LIBERIA:

According to the US State Department, Liberia was considered to be a hardship post. Disease was rampant. Unsuspecting healthy looking people would arrive daily at Robertsfield from the United States or Europe. Within a couple of weeks, they would be seen, pale and wan, at the doctor's office. I had the misfortune to contract infectious hepatitis; my skin and the whites of my eyes yellowed. Blessedly, the children and Doug remained healthy during our entire stay. Along with the threat of hepatitis, there were also malaria, sleeping sickness, and leprosy, to name a few of the diseases lurking in the shadows ready to pounce on one. I was ordered to bed for a couple of weeks. The only food I was allowed to eat had to be boiled and fat free. I'm sure you can imagine how appetizing the sight of boiled liver can be? It takes on a blue hue. Ugh!

Jeff, Janet and I in front of our house in Liberia, West Africa (1958)

During my convalescence, Chio, our laundry boy, knocked on the door of my bedroom. "Come in --- oh, how are you Chio? --- nice to see you," I said with a smile. "Oh Missy, Missy!" Chio moaned. "I in trouble! --- the police outside waiting for me, Missy." "What happened Chio?" I anxiously asked. Chio walked a few steps closer to me and said, "Oh Missy, der a girl in de village next door, she very pretty Missy but she married.

Jeff and Janet going native in Liberia, West Africa (1958)

--- I just fool with her a little bit Missy --- her husband find out and want money. Missy --- I just fool with her a little --- I didn't do it good! --- Can you give me an advance on my pay?" I interrogated him a bit more before saying, "Yes." Liberians mostly answer "Yes" by simply inhaling fast. I continued, "The girl is in the next village, you say?" Chio gasped. "The police are here to take you away?" He inhaled a "Yes" again. "You just fooled with her?" He nodded and gasped once more. "You didn't do it good?" He could hardly contain himself and nervously blurted out loudly, "No Missy!" I finished questioning him with: "---and you have to give her husband money? --- hmm --- I think you ought to go back and DO IT GOOD!" Chio, at long last, caught the humor in the drift of my questioning, grinned and quickly said, "Aw Missy make joke!" Then he laughed uncontrollably out loud. Money in hand, Chio left my bedroom a much happier fellow. He could now pay his way out of his predicament.

## THE NO FRIENDS OF MUSIC:

Back home in Connecticut, we had socialized with a group of friends who were interested in all forms of music. We came to be known as "The No Friends of Music." Meetings were generally held once a month. In our new Liberian home, we met more and more people who both enjoyed one another's company and were interested in the arts. Based on our Connecticut experience, I started a similar "No Friends" group in Liberia. Since Doug and I had brought several recordings with us from Connecticut, we decided to have the first meeting at our house. A lively discussion ensued after listening to Puccini's beautiful opera, _Madame Butterfly_.

At another meeting, the subject was "The No Friends of Pigmy Hippopotamus Hunting." A zoologist came and talked about the intricacies of capturing one alive. I had no idea that these mammals were only to be found in Liberia and nowhere else in the world. Of all the meetings, my favorite was that at which three male Lebanese shopkeepers offered to show us the art of Lebanese "belly dancing." They arrived carrying their multi-colored scarves and recorded dance music. I thought only women indulged in this dance but soon found out that men were just as good at it, if not better. They certainly did themselves proud doing a modified version of wiggle, jiggle, bump and grind.

## SHARING THE SOUNDS OF LIBERIA WITH MY PARENTS:

One sunny day, some toe tapping, hand clapping music demanded my complete attention. It first seeped into our home as a far away faint sound, then became louder and louder. I went to find John in the kitchen and asked if there was a party going on outside? He said: "No Missy, somebody die in village. Music play to ask spirit to leave and not stay around." I had wanted for some time to share my Liberian experience with my parents in the United States, and this was my chance. I searched for my tape recorder, found it, and hung the microphone out the window to catch the wonderful music.  When the sounds began to fade, I pulled the mike back in.

I continued recording on this tape the familiar daily sounds I heard, such as our dog barking, Jeff playing the African drum, and Janet crying.  (I must admit I did pinch her in order to achieve that effect.)  I mailed the tape to Plainfield, New Jersey with a note asking my parents to send back a tape of programs I so sorely missed, including the Mormon Tabernacle Choir, Dad playing jazz on the piano and my favorite radio programs.  They responded by return mail.  It gave Doug and me esthetic joy to hear what they taped and sent back, which so poignantly reminded us of home.

**Janet's first passport (1958)**

Betty Jones

## RETURNING HOME TO CONNECTICUT:

In 1958 after almost two and a half years, Doug's projects were rapidly coming to an end. The promised new water filtration plant for Monrovia was operable and traffic was finally using the road connecting Liberia with Sierra Leone. On our last day in our beautiful, well kept house, the barefoot houseboys lined up in front of Doug and me to say goodbye. John, the cook, stepped forward to speak for himself and the others. He was proudly wearing one of my cast off maternity tops I had given him to replace his worn out usual outfit. Imploringly he asked, "You mus' leave Janet with we Missy. She part of we. Janet, Liberian! We raise her good and get fine bride price." The other boys nodded in agreement. I replied, "Thank you, John for your offer. I'm sure you would raise her good but I'm sorry to say, we're taking her with us." Doug and I bid them our heartfelt farewells, then got into the waiting car and whizzed off to the airport. Once in the air, I began to ruminate on the intriguing experiences I had been fortunate enough to have had during our stay in Liberia. As I settled comfortably into my seat for the long flight home, waves of nostalgic memories of Wilton washed over me. I happily drifted off to sleep and dreamed of our fun times and the many friends we had made and would miss in Liberia.

# Wilton Playshop

After many long hours in the air on our return trip to the United States, we were overjoyed to finally turn into our own driveway. While in Africa, we had rented the house out completely furnished for almost 2-1/2 years. As our eyes further focused on our home and lawn, we were stunned to see that the grass was almost hip high. It seemed as though it had not been cut in quite some time. Doug reasoned sadly, "I guess the tenants didn't attend to their regular yard maintenance chores as we had thought they would." Approaching the front door, we were equally shocked to find it unlocked and standing wide open. Since we knew the tenants had moved out weeks earlier, with some trepidation we entered our home and in unison heaved a sigh of relief to find all our things just about as we had left them. This all occurred long before illicit, drug-inspired robberies began to be committed. In fact, Wilton had no police force. Only one Resident State Trooper, Bill Quaintance, patrolled the entire town and he was all Wilton needed at the time.

It was gratifying to once again resume my responsibilities as housewife and mother: to clean the house, do laundry and cook the meals myself. All of these duties gave me a renewed sense of soul felt satisfaction. There were no houseboys to do these chores or to catch a glimpse of me streaking nakedly from the bedroom to the bathroom, hoping to be invisible. So daily I rendered unto Caesar what was Caesar's, but after sundown, was my time to follow my heart's desire ---- music.

At that time, I went down to The Wilton Playshop, the same place where I had sung _The Medium_, and auditioned for their upcoming show. They were casting Arthur Miller's _The Crucible_, and I was assigned the role of Tituba. The play dealt with the Salem witch hunts. I felt strange speaking my lines and not singing them. As soon as the show's run was over, I

61

auditioned for the musical _Pal Joey_ by Rogers and Hart. A sassy Richard Rogers tune, "The Lady is a Tramp," was written into the show's night club scene especially for me. It was my first experience singing a Broadway tune. However, singing just one song only whetted my appetite for taking on a proper musical role of more substance.

By this time The Playshop knew what I could do artistically, so I did not have to audition. A few dramatic plays intervened, then _Once Upon A Mattress_ was next on the docket. It was based on the mythical story of The _Princess and the Pea_ and featured music by Mary Rodgers, Richard Rodgers's daughter. The role of the Minstrel was originally written for the tenor voice. Good tenors are rare birds to find, so I was given the role and had to learn how to play a man but sing the music up in the soprano register. The director painstakingly showed me how to convincingly move and walk. After one performance in particular, I changed from the Minstrel man's costume into my dress and came down from the upstairs dressing rooms along with the rest of the cast, ready to greet the enthusiastic audience in the Green Room. A young boy ran up to me exclaiming loudly in disbelieving wonderment, "But, you're a girl --- you're not a guy!"

Even though I eventually enjoyed playing the Minstrel, I had originally yearned for the part of Queen Aggravain, the dangerous manipulator. It was a much bigger role. My cousin Jane White had played it on Broadway opposite Carol Burnett. The dramatic lessons learned as the Playshop's Minstrel, nevertheless, stood me in good stead. Years later when I sang the very demanding pants role of Leonora in Beethoven's _Fidelio_, a reviewer from England's Opera Magazine said of my performance: "Betty Jones was the most believable woman I've ever seen playing a man."

## SOUTH PACIFIC:
In 1962, I was totally blissed out with excitement to learn that I had been cast by The Wilton Playshop to play Bloody Mary

in _South Pacific._ Juanita Hall had originally played the role on Broadway. She was of mixed lineage including African-American, but the character she portrayed was supposed to be Tonganese. Up until the show's Broadway opening in 1949, black people were only stereotyped as menials or buffoons. Rodgers and Hammerstein permanently changed the course of musical theatre as it had been known in the past. Performers "of color" were now free to be cast as characters of other races. _South Pacific_ could boast being the first show ever in theatrical history to integrate the chorus, singers, dancers and actors.

At one of the early Wilton Playshop rehearsals, I was given my costume for the first time. It was a bright floral printed "muu-muu" with beads to match. I carried the dress up the creaking stairs to the curtained balcony dressing room which, I had completely forgotten, had no walls or dividing curtain to afford even a modest privacy for me and my colleagues of different sexes. Many community theater groups had similar arrangements. On the positive side, if one ever wanted to check out someone in every way possible, this was the golden opportunity.

I, as Bloody Mary, had quite a job ahead of me. After returning from Africa as a second time new Mom, I had slimmed way down, but my character was supposed to be quite overweight. I solved the problem by teaching myself how to temporarily realign my spine so that my stomach jutted forward and filled out the front of my "muu-muu," making the illusion of obesity a believable reality.

In the show, a representation of a kiosk was built on stage. From this I was to sell my tourist memorabilia, consisting of grass skirts, boar's-tooth bracelets, and shrunken heads. I learned during rehearsals how to speak broken English. When I was asked by interested servicemen about the price of my merchandise, my usual reply was, "Fo dolla" or "Ten dolla." A boar's-tooth bracelet was, "Hundred dolla." One fellow asked me, "Why is the shrunken head so small?" I answered in a matter of fact manner, "Shlunk!" as I sneered at him, behind my smile, because of his seeming stupidity. Squeezing the head between my hands I continued, "Only way to keep human head is to shlink em." To my surprise, the serviceman turned to leave. I tried to stop him by shouting, "Where you go? --- Come back! --- Cheapskate! --- Crummy GI! --- Sadsack! --- Droopy Drawers! --- Stingy Bastard!" The guy fast disappeared into the wings of the stage. Bending forward, I broke, as the script demanded, into peals of uncontrolable laughter.

In the show, Bloody Mary is quite taken by the handsome and charming Lieutenant Cable. Her hidden agenda is to introduce him into the life of her beautiful daughter, Liat. There is only one hitch. Liat lives on Bali Ha'i, the next in a chain of South Sea Islands. One can actually see its peak only a short distance away by boat. Bloody Mary sings about Bali Ha'i in the hopes of enticing Cable to go there and get to know Liat:

".... Some day you'll see me, floating in the sunshine,
my head sticking out from a low flying cloud.
You'll hear me call you, singing thru the sunshine,
sweet and clear as can be. Come to me, here am I
come to me. If you try, you'll find me --
where the sky meets the sea.
Here am I, your special island,
Come to me! come to me!
Bali Ha'i, Bali Ha'i, Bali Ha'i....."

Generally, if the music and lyrics are well written and I have done my homework, I will actually see a video in my mind's eye, all in color, conjured up by the word pictures of the song or aria. Untinkered with, I then pass these visual sensations on directly to the audience.

Just as Mary had hoped, Liat and Cable fall delightfully in love at their first meeting, but Cable decides, because of the then forbidden mixing of the races, not to pursue the relationship any further. He is sent on a dangerous mission and is killed.

A parallel relationship develops between Emile deBecque, a middle aged French planter, and the high spirited Ensign Nellie Forbush from Arkansas. DeBeque was married to a Polynesian who died a long time ago and is now raising their two children. He sings the show stopper, "Some Enchanted Evening." The words, "Once you have found her, never let her go," give the audience insight into his deepening feelings for Nellie. She is enchanted with deBecque but realizes, after seeing pictures of his children, that they are of mixed heritage. This fact almost brings an end to their budding romance. Angrily, she sings as she showers, "I'm going to wash that man right out of my hair."

## COMMUNITY THEATER ANTICS:
One night during a _South Pacific_ rehearsal, directly in front of me some four feet away stood the singer who was playing the role of Emile deBecque. He was listening for his stage entrance cue. His back was towards me and he clasped and unclasped his hands behind him. At regular intervals, he seemed to glance fleetingly back at me, re-adjust his hand height, then face the lights on the stage again. All of a sudden he backed quickly away from the lights directly into me, his hands finding the furry spot they sought. I let out a surprised cry as he, with a smile, slipped un-noticed into the shadows. I vowed then and there to repay him in kind at the first possible chance.

At a private party later that evening, one of the guests added to the levity by producing some very naughty cards. I blinked disbelievingly as I thumbed through them. Here was an unclothed man whose face looked for all the world just like deBecque being pleasured with whipped cream by two similarly unclothed gorgeous girls. A figurative 200 watt bulb turned on over my head, brightening my inner maniacal grin. I begged the owner of the cards to give me a few. My wish was immediately granted. I knew exactly what I was going to do with them.

In one scene, Emile deBecque shares pictures of his two racially mixed children with his new love interest, Nellie Forbush. Only moments before that scene, during a rehearsal when no one was looking, I exchanged the naughty cards for the legitimate photographs. Finally, the dialogue on stage arrived at the point in the script where Emile takes his children's photographs out of his pocket. The Emile in our show glanced down at them momentarily as he prepared to proudly show them to Nellie. It took only a split second for him to do a classic double take as he registered what he saw. His eyes bulged out of their sockets in disbelief and his mouth gaped open with surprise. Stammering a bit, he made up a few lines while secretly tucking the pictures safely back in his pocket.

I purposely chose a rehearsal to get creative and repay the singer who had molested me. A performance is sacred. Also I have not divulged his identity in order to protect his good name. We were friends and colleagues before performing in _South Pacific_ and continued to be friends after that "tit for tat" incident and until his sad untimely death.

As the show roared to its successful conclusion, I was well aware that I would miss playing the conniving, loud mouth, betel nut chewing Bloody Mary and also the cast members who after a time had begun to feel like family. To fill the void when it was over, Doug took me to Hawaii to visit his cousin Bill, a retired Marine Sargeant Major. While there, we visited the Island of Kauai and went to some of the local watering holes. There we were introduced to many native Hawaians who welcomed us warmly. On one of our sightseeing jaunts, the car we rode in protested the steep incline by sputtering and straining uphill until we reached the top of a    tall mountain.   A restaurant on the peak provided us with a delicious lunch.

Before returning to sea level, Doug's cousin encouraged us to follow him out onto the stone patio to see the view.   Lush verdant vegetation sloped precipitously down to the electric blue ocean far below.   Bill told us that the movie South Pacific had been filmed there in the 50's.   It starred Rossano Brazzi, Mitzi Gaynor, John Kerr and Ray Walston.   Opera singer, Giorgio Tozzi 's voice sang the role of Emile deBecque.   Following Doug's cousin's index finger's directive to the spot below where the land meets the sea, I began to hear snatches of music playing in my head and felt a glowing warm sense of kinship for this place.   Bloody Mary was finally home.

## DARIEN DINNER THEATER:

In 1993, Connecticut's Darien Dinner Theater decided to revive _South Pacific_, so I had another opportunity to experience the character of Bloody Mary 30 years after first playing the role at the Wilton Playshop.   This was not "little theater" but a professional production.   Everyone in the show could boast of many past theater and television credits. Jamie Farr of "MASH" fame   brilliantly played the character Luther Billis.   Billis was a manipulator, as was Bloody Mary.   Both dealt in souvenirs and would go to great lengths to get what they wanted.     I still remember feeling a little intimidated performing with such a fine experienced actor as Farr, although I had by this time sung major operatic roles on many of the great stages of the world.   Bloody Mary's personality grew, both in depth and dimension, because of the unique way that Jamie delivered his lines to me.   I also believe in retrospect that the entire cast similarly benefited from his presence on stage and the high caliber of his professional expertise.

DARIEN, CT.---ACTOR JAMIE FARR (KLINGER ON T-V's M*A*S*H)
AS "LUTHER BILLIS" DOES BUSINESS WITH CONNECTICUT'S OWN
BETTY JONES, AS "BLOODY MARY" IN RODGERS AND HAMMERSTEIN'S
SOUTH PACIFIC AT CLUB CAROUSEL THROUGH NOV. 7th.

**Darien Dinner Theater (1993)**

# Early Performances

## THE SINGING LADY:

Experiences in early childhood can serve, in part, to familiarize one with what he will need to succeed in later life. Saturday mornings one could always find prepubescent me, sitting cross legged on the living room floor in front of the radio, waiting patiently to hear my favorite of all programs, "The Singing Lady" with Ireene Wicker. Miss Wicker wrote her own scripts, composed the music she sang, and was a brilliant monologist. She would change the range of her voice to fit any character. When needed, she could sound much like a man. The usual children's story repertoire such as _Rapunzel_, _Snow White_, _Pinocchio_, and the like took on new meaning when I realized she was the only performer on the show, except for the excellent pianist Samuel Sanders, who accompanied her when she sang. Presenting the life stories of famous composers, including those from Russia, was another one of her specialties. During the era of the infamous McCarthy Communist "Witch Hunt," all of a sudden she was off the air.

From my early days as a camp counselor and through working at a day care center, my special soul fulfilling joy came from performing for live, responsive audiences of children. I put together shows during which I sang folk songs while accompanying myself on the guitar. I seemed to know instinctively what was needed because of the many hours spent listening to "The Singing Lady."

I was overjoyed, one Saturday morning, to hear "The Singing Lady" was back on radio. Searching for a pencil, I wrote down where to get in touch with Miss Wicker. My introductory letter praised her as the one responsible for helping me set my life's course in the musical entertainment field. A few days after mailing my congratulatory epistle, my phone rang. A Wilton neighbor named Nancy Taffel was on the line. She blurted out, "My mother asked me to call and tell you that she loved your letter! When I told her you were a wonderful folk singer, she asked if you would come to New York and sing on her radio program." I replied with a surprised smile in my voice, "I'd love to!" Nancy then passed on to me the when and where details for me to jot down.

I spent the week before my appearance on the show choosing what I was going to sing and practicing it. I even took some additional guitar lessons. When the big day finally arrived, I hopped aboard the train to New York City, quietly strumming and humming all the way. Intermittently, my thoughts fabricated a scenario how Miss Wicker had fared during her banishment years. I said to myself, "She's probably seen better days. Are her clothes worn and frayed? I'll soon know."

As I entered the radio studio, a petite woman with an attractive blonde page boy cut and doe eyes greeted me. "You must be Betty Jones. I'm Ireene Wicker. My daughter Nancy lives in Wilton, too, as you know. She told me you were beautiful and tall. You are just as she described you." She extended her small hand, which disappeared into mine as we shook hands. "Come," she continued, "Let me show you the stool you'll sit on and the mike you'll sing into. It's almost time. Get out your guitar" I did as she requested and all went exceedingly well.

When the show was over, I was thanked enthusiastically by The Singing Lady and her crew. She then invited Doug and me for dinner, set a date and gave me her address written on a folded-up piece of paper. I did not read it until I was on the return train back to Connecticut. "What!" I exclaimed loudly when I read it. Many of my fellow passengers turned and stared at me. Their startled look matched mine perfectly. The woman I thought, before meeting her, might be financially a little worse for wear, lived at a very fashionable

Fifth Avenue address. Her last name was not Wicker but Hammer, Mrs. Victor Hammer. A bell chimed in my mind at the thought of that name. When I was studying art at Sarah Lawrence College, I frequented numerous art galleries in New York City. A flash back memory reminded me that on one of my many gallery pilgrimages, I visited the Hammer Galleries on 57th Street owned by Victor and his brother Armand Hammer. Armand at that time was the founder and CEO of Occidental Petroleum Corp. "Wow!" I whispered to myself.

When Doug and I arrived at their apartment house for dinner, the doorman already knew our names and ushered us right in. He also must have alerted our host and hostess, because when we stepped off the elevator their door was open and they stood smilingly waiting to welcome us. I was duly impressed as I scanned their tastefully decorated, spacious apartment. After polite, interesting conversation over cocktails and dinner in the dining room, we moved back into the living room for coffee and dessert. I espied the familiar curved form of a guitar leaning against the wall. I asked, "Who plays the 12 string guitar?" Victor answered, "I do but its not mine. It belongs to the actor Theodore Bikel. He left it here. If you'd like to sing a folk song I know, I'd love to accompany you." I nodded, "Yes," and asked, "Do you know 'Go tell Aunt Rhody?' Picking up the guitar, he settled himself in an easy chair. "Sure do," he replied as he began to strum it. I sang;

> "Go tell Aunt Rhody,
> Go tell Aunt Rhody,
> Go tell Aunt Rhody,
> that the old grey goose is dead."

> "She died in the mill pond,
> She died in the mill pond,
> She died in the mill pond,
> a standing on her head"

This was one song among many that I sang to children when entertaining them. They loved to hear it and also to sing it. When I finished singing, Victor, Ireene, and my husband all surprised me by clapping and cheering. I was touched and pleased when, after hearing me, the Hammers asked if I would consider singing at their private club, the very elite Lotos Club. To be heard on radio is one thing, but to appear and perform in New York for the intelligentsia and be commensurately paid was beyond my wildest dreams.

I later found out that "The Singing Lady" had won every award offered for children's programs, including the Peabody Award and the Parents Magazine Award. Ireene has had her books published and has written three operas and a series of plays with music, all for children. Fate once again dealt me an unforeseeably delightful experience. Ireene Wicker, the unique trailblazer, while tracing her steps along life's path, had encouraged me to attempt a musical hike to higher ground, if and when the chance presented itself.

## THE NOT SO PERFECT PRINCESS:

My love of performing for children became further evident when I was asked in 1961 by Connecticut's Westport Community Theater to perform in and co-author a children's musical called "The Not So Perfect Princess". My friend and collaborator, Bunni Singer, wrote the text and lyrics. I was in charge of writing the music, which included an overture, songs for the three sprites who doubled as pages and, of course, the princess. The music for the character Pan (half man/half goat) I farmed out to Alice

Westport, Connecticut (1961)

72

Valkenburgh because I wanted it written in the impressionist's whole tone scale, like the music of Debussy. It was too difficult for me to compose without having studied theory. Julie Anderson, who became my accompanist, also helped write some of the music.

I particularly enjoyed writing the witch's song called "Mopsa's Lament." I looked forward to playing the witch, singing and hamming it up. Mopsa feels she is a misunderstood witch. The first verse of the lament provides a clue as to her plight. It is written in the sad key of "G" minor.

"Have pity on the poor old witch, you always say I'm bad.
There's a wicked one in every tale which really is so sad.
'Cause witches are like anyone as you can plainly see.
There's a bit of witch in all of us, so sing along with me."

The audience of children and parents were encouraged at this point to sing the refrain along with me:

"Hocus pocus, Dom-in-ocus, Abra-cadabra too! These are magic words we sing when mixing witches brew."

A long black dress was Mopsa's costume and an ordinary old fashioned kitchen mop was her wig. I borrowed my husband's white tennis shoes (size 12) which I wore on the wrong feet so that they comically faced away from each other and curled upward at the toes. I played Mopsa as a clown/witch. My spell casting wand was another wood handled mop. Everyone in the show had to have the talent and experience to both sing and dance. When the audience reacted, it was very important to know how to hold whatever position we were in at that moment, until the laughter and applause died down, before continuing. I wisely wrote the music so that it lay in the mid-vocal range. There were no operatic high notes to demand that one scale their treacherous heights.

In one scene near the end of the show, when I was being taunted by the sprites, my voluminous underpants fall to the floor on cue. They were made of white satin material with large red polka dots all over them. The sprites pointed at me accusingly and screamed gleefully, "You lost your pants, you lost your pants!" Mopsa, not hearing them correctly, nervously inspected and impulsively brushed off her dress. With equal fervor she blasted back at them, "Ants! Ants! Where are the ants?" In preparation for this on-stage antic, I had to make sure my thumb nail was of sufficient length to be able on cue to undo the only snap holding up my pants.

When my parents came to see the show, Dad was shocked to witness my pants falling down in public. Embarrassed, he seemed to turn the thought over in his mind and came to the conclusion, "Oh, those bloomers are too big for her anyway. I guess it's part of the show." The audience was convulsed with laughter, and Dad then joined them.

We only performed on weekends. Every night at the end of the show, I got a chance to meet the members of the audience when they filed out of the theater. As the children passed by me, they delighted in singing "Hocus Pocus" back to me. Some had convinced themselves that these words really made it possible for them to cast a spell. I gave each child in turn a luscious lollipop and lovingly waved goodbye.

## FIRST ACCOMPANISTS:
It is my firm belief that the blade of grass right next to the toe, as one walks life's lawn, is more important to one's present and future than anything that exists on the other side of the fence. Children were my very first audiences in Wilton.

First Accompanist -Julie Anderson

I sang folk songs and accompanied myself on the guitar. Since my knowledge of this instrument was rudimentary, I decided that I could present a wider range of selections if I were accompanied on the piano. Where to find an accompanist? Every Thursday evening I attended choir rehearsal at the Wilton Congregational Church. I asked an attractive blond, who always sat next to me in the alto section, if she knew of anyone who accompanied singers. "I can accompany you," she said brightly. "I majored in music at Vassar." From then on Julie Anderson and Betty Jones were an inseparable duo in performing operatic arias, light classics and even Broadway show songs, for every age group. I certainly got the experience I sought, thanks to her. In addition to playing for me, Julie also accompanied many of the Wilton Playshop musicals as well as the annual Christmas Eve gathering and carol sing at the Wilton Creche.

My winning streak continued on and on, carrying me to unanticipated heights. Don Comrie, a retired opera coach from the Manhattan School of Music, took an undying interest in me as a performer and singer. Together with my voice teacher, Don became responsible for the polishing of my craft, in every aspect, to a very high gloss. He was a Wilton neighbor and an excellent accompanist, and he became my private coach. He asked no recompense but joyfully shared his knowledge of song, oratorio and opera literature. He often phoned me on the spur of the moment. I would answer and say "Hello?" Don's voice on the other end of the line, most times, would say, "If it's all right with you, I'll be right over. I've just run across some interesting music I think you should hear and perhaps learn." I would warmly welcome Don when he arrived as he headed straight for the piano and placed the music he had brought on the rack. When Don played, it was as though he was carefully unfurling, in sound, precious bolts of musical material, some of which were sensuously silken in texture and design. Others were touchingly sad, in pale blue velvet or, in contrast, bright red and energizingly rhythmic. Because of him, my repertoire grew to include French songs by Debussy and Poulenc; German Lieder; the music of the Spanish composer, de Falla; opera arias by Wagner, Verdi, and Puccini; songs in Yiddish and Hebrew; songs from Gershwin's *Porgy and Bess*; spirituals; and numerous Broadway tunes.

Through Don, I learned the melodies and the composer's dynamics, quiet here, swell to loud there, faster here and slower there, but how was I to learn to convincingly pronounce all those foreign languages? Wilton's Continuing Education offered many of them that I sought, so I signed up and went to school in the evenings. I discovered an important short cut, when trying to memorize words in a language not my own. I found that it quickened the process, If I did not, in order to understand the meaning, just translate the words into English but also drew a representational picture above the foreign words in question. This mind trick brings meaning alive for both the singer and also the audience, because one begins to think in a new language.

Don and I put together and performed many a successful concert, including a Candlelight Concert at the Wilton Congregational Church.  I was the first singer asked to sing on the Candlelight series, which until then had featured only instrumentalists.

## REDDING CHORAL SOCIETY:
Like dropping a proverbial pebble into a still pond, my fame preceded me in an ever widening word-of-mouth circle.  The Redding Choral Society engaged me to be soloist in Handel's *Messiah* and other oratorios.  Their capable conductor, Clois Ensor, was a small, balding, ruddy faced gentleman with silky white hair, what he had left of it.  As I looked down at him from my tall perspective, I could not help but think how much he resembled one of the charming seven dwarfs in the "Snow White" fantasy.  Besides his attracting good choral singers, Clois always managed to put together a small orchestra to accompany them in concert.  In those days, I was still an alto.  I made the transition to soprano during this time period.

My next concert, held in September 1963, was *King David* by the modernist Honneger. Clois arrived at our house from Redding to give me a foretaste of the music.  While there, he saw a young boy streak by the window.  He asked, "Who's that?" I answered, "Oh him?  He's our son Jeff." He then lamented, "We can't find anyone to cast as King David when he was a young boy, as demanded by the composer.  Does Jeff sing?" "Oh yes," I replied, "quite sweetly too!" Excited by the thought that his problem might be shortly resolved, he said, "Get him to come in and let me hear him." Clois was positively impressed and Jeff was invited to make his musical debut, singing the role of King David as a boy.

All went well during the performance until the time came for the soloists, including Jeff, to take their bows at the end. He was no where to be found, until someone happened to look outside and saw him climbing a tree.  He ran back and re-entered the concert hall, arriving only seconds before it was his turn to bow. As he bent over and bowed, I was horrified to see that he had been rolling in freshly cut grass. His hair was covered with green blades and his shirt had come out of the back of his pants and was flapping freely in the breeze. As the great Fats Waller wisely said, "One never know --- do one." Life is full of unanticipated surprises.

## DANBURY SYMPHONY:

I was surprised to learn that Clois was a member of the Danbury Symphony. He spoke glowingly about me to their conductor, John Burnett. I had always longed to feel the thrill of singing with a symphony orchestra. Thanks to Clois, it began to look like I was going to get the chance.

Sure enough, in a few days, the phone rang. It was a call from the conductor, John Burnett, asking if I would like to sing with the orchestra. He wanted to know as soon as possible what I would like to sing. I replied, "Yes," excitedly, thanked him and said, "I'll call you back with the possible repertoire". I searched for pieces that I had worked on with Don Comrie and had previously sung in numerous recitals. Thank goodness for the local churches, temples and musical organizations like the Schubert Musical Society, South Shore Music Club and others. My concert songs, lieder and arias had been given a chance to break in and be comfortable like a good pair of old shoes. In determining what to sing, one always has to make sure that he chooses the best opening number one can find and that all the subsequent works are in different keys. In addition, they should progressively move from the more complicated to the simpler and the dates should be in chronological order of composition.

I decided on the songs I would sing with the Symphony and communicated my choice to John Burnett. In a shorter time than I thought it was possible for them to obtain the music, I was called to a rehearsal. I arrived before the orchestra had tuned up. Orchestras tune their instruments to one note, a

"Concert A." This note vibrates at 440 cycles per second. The "A" in the United States is fewer cycles per second than the one set by musicians in Europe, so when one is singing an aria overseas, one always sings at a slightly higher pitch.

John Burnett introduced himself to me and in turn presented me to the orchestra. It was a good thing that he stood on a podium. He was so short that, without it, he would have disappeared behind the music stand while conducting. Before tuning up, musicians cleaned their instruments and thoroughly checked them out. Because the woodwind and brass instruments are blown, saliva tends to collect in them. Every instrument has a release valve, to let the unwanted moisture out. The only musician I knew socially was Bob, the oboe player. We waved at each other fast and furiously and flashed reciprocal wall to wall smiles. I watched as he resumed the care and cleaning of his instrument, but his eyes seemed to be magnetically riveted to mine. He took off the oboe's mouthpiece and picked up a special string which was weighted on one end. Dropping the weight down the length of his instrument, he pulled the string up and down and winked at me as he did so. In response, I laughed as quietly as I could, while trying to catch my breath between silent guffaws.

My friend's tomfoolery, the moment before I sang, was heaven sent. Even a simple rehearsal without an audience has the capacity to send the adrenalin coursing through the blood, agitating the nerve cell receptors. Humor, like meditation, has a calming capacity, bringing the thoughts into the present instead of fixating fearfully on what might transpire in the future. As the rehearsal progressed, I relaxed and was then in a good frame of mind to really enjoy performing.

What to wear? One wants the audience to concentrate on one's face, so I chose from my wardrobe, a long dress that covered almost everything but my hands and facial expressions. Material wise, it was a sparkler! Evidently, my first appearance with a symphony orchestra went well, because on February 27, 1964 the Westport Town Crier wrote this about my performance:

".....The high-water mark for professionalism and polish in the program undoubtedly was the singing of Betty Jones. A resident of Wilton, she has a countywide following of admirers aware of her musical versatility. Whether as an earthy "Bloody Mary" in South Pacific, as the theatrically operatic lead in _The Medium_, or an oratorio and church soloist, or as composer and performer of children's musical plays, her brilliant and beautifully controlled soprano has repeatedly delighted appreciative local audiences.

On Sunday she took on still another role, interpreting two of the greatest French art songs..."Villanelle" and "The Spectre of the Rose" by Berlioz, set to poems by Gautier. Her voice projected effortlessly, the lyrical sensuousness of these     lovely songs, and seemed equally at home in the darkly melancholy, blues like quality of 'Summertime' and 'My Man's Gone Now' from Gershwin's _Porgy  and Bess_...."

## CONCERT ARTISTS GUILD AWARD:

"Hi there!" a beautifully placed male voice said when I picked up the phone receiver. "It's Paul Kwartin." (Paul had sung with me in _The Medium_ at the Wilton Playshop). "I just wanted to tell you that I was so proud to be in the audience at your "Lado Musicale" concert Wednesday in New York. I couldn't come backstage after the concert to see you, because I had to get right back to the office. My uncle who sits on the Kosciuszko Foundation Board brought me. They were financially responsible for the hall and publicity, but you made it the total success that it was. What fun to hear you sing again. You were absolutely wonderful! I'm so excited about your progress, both vocally and dramatically. Betty, you are now a polished performer and I think it's time you thought seriously about an operatic career. Your 'Dich theure Halle' from _Tannhäuser_ was by far the best I've heard in a long time."

After a short pause, he then said, "I know of an important audition coming up soon that will interest you. The Concert Artists Guild is sponsoring a competition for young singers. The prize is a solo concert at Carnegie Recital Hall. If you win, the entire music world will hear about Betty Jones. I've already talked to my cousin, the opera singer Evelyn Lear, about you, and she has promised to shepherd your application through the process. Since you are probably past the age limit for the competition, whatever you do, never show anyone your birth certificate." I interrupted shouting joyfully, "Oh thank you! thank you Paul!" He continued, "So expect the application in the mail and follow through. I also have some influential friends at the Met. I'll see what I can do for you there. Lets get at it Betty! Let me know how things go. Good luck and cheerie bye." As soon as he hung up, I burst into tears of joy and let out an ionospheric shattering cry of ecstatic hopefulness.

Paul was as good as his word. Not only did I win the 1969 Concert Artists Guild Award and was awarded the opportunity to perform at Carnegie Recital Hall but I also auditioned and received the Alice Turney Long Grant from the Metropolitan Opera Association. That helped me financially, to continue my vocal studies. The Met insisted however, that I work with a teacher of their choosing, Madame Marinka Gurevich. At that particular time she was teaching, among other well known singers, Roberta Peters and Martina Arroyo.

My usual accompanist and teacher, Gibner King, was not very happy about my studying with Madame Gurevich, but I had to do what I thought was best for me and my career, and I searched for someone to accompany my upcoming Carnegie Recital Hall Concert. A Connecticut pianist by the name of

Elmar Burrows jumped into the breech and together we prepared some twenty pieces, starting off with an aria by Handel, "Piangero la sorte mia" from *Julius Caesar*. We rehearsed all the songs and arias until we were satisfied they were ready for the concert, but then he dropped a bomb on me! At the beginning of what I thought was to be a rehearsal, he said sadly, "Betty, I've just been offered a position on the Music Faculty at Indiana University. I'm very sorry to tell you that I won't be able to play your debut concert in New York. Please forgive me! I'm leaving for Indiana as soon as possible." He gave me a hug, wished me good luck and left.

I rushed to the phone to call Paul Kwartin. His response was, "Don't worry Betty, calm down! I know another accompanist who can support you and be sensitive to your every musical need. His name is Herbert Mayer. He lives in New York City, has played for me on occasion and is very good. I'll give him a call to prepare the way for you. You call him tonight after I've talked to him and set up a rehearsal schedule." "Oh Paul," I stammered, "how can I ever repay you?" He replied soothingly, "Just sing like the angel you are, and all will be well."

Herbert Mayer, the pianist Paul suggested, proved to be every bit as good as predicted. The first thing we did at rehearsal was to rearrange the order of all the songs and arias. I would still open with the Handel aria in Italian, but after that I would sing four German Lieder by Brahms. Next, I would share with the audience songs in Italian and two Puccini arias, also in Italian. After a short intermission, I would move on into French. We planned to perform two beautiful songs by Faure and Berlioz, lightening up with the charming songs by Poulenc, "C" and "Les Gars qui vont a la Fete." At this point in the program, the concert would end with four songs in English, the last being Gershwin's "My Man's Gone Now" from *Porgy and Bess.*

As one sticks the big toe into the blue swimming pool water to see how cold it is before jumping in, I had the opportunity to do a complete dry run of my concert with my new accompanist at Emanuel Episcopal Church in Weston, Connecticut. It was a blessing to be able to test my wings singing the exact same material I would sing in my debut concert only five days later.

I was thrilled after much rehearsing to at long last be singing at Carnegie Recital Hall on the evening of March 25th 1969. Two bus loads of family and friends came down from Connecticut to support me. When I walked out on stage, I was greeted with smiles and applause. I instantly went into automatic overdrive and the concert went swimmingly well, seeming to sing itself. The next day, a review of the concert appeared in the New York Times. The headline read: "ENTHUSIASTIC HOUSE HEARS BETTY JONES." It went on to say:

> "....not many singers count themselves lucky enough to walk onto a New York stage and be greeted by a sold out house as was Betty Jones last night in Carnegie Recital Hall. The hall was packed with attentive but demonstrative people who seemed to regard her as an old friend. On the basis of her personality, one can see why. Miss Jones is tall and strikingly good looking with one of those personalities that go zinging over the footlights and hit the audience right between the eyes...."

Betty Jones

**Carnegie Recital Hall Concert - New York (1969)**

**Carnegie Recital Hall Concert - New York (1969)**

84

# Boston Pops

Approximately two months after my successful Carnegie Recital Hall Concert, I received a telephone call from one of my Sarah Lawrence College classmates, Marcia Zonis, who lived in Boston. She asked that I immediately send her biographical material about my current career. It seemed her husband Mort was on a Committee planning the 25th Reunion for Harvard's Class of 1945 to be held June 1970. The highlight of the Reunion Week was to be "A Night at the Pops" in Boston's Symphony Hall. His Committee was to select subject to approval by the conductor, Arthur Fiedler, the soloists for the evening.

To my surprise, I learned that Marcia had traveled down to New York to hear my Carnegie Recital Hall Concert. During our college years, she had always been thrilled by my singing. I was truly touched to find tears of joy in her eyes when she greeted and hugged me backstage after my performance. Unknown to me, she prevailed on Mort to submit my name as one of the Pops soloists. I had no idea what was brewing in Boston and how it would affect my life, but I was soon to find out. Forthwith I was informed of my future good fortune by being asked to come to Boston to meet and sing for Arthur Fiedler.

When I knocked, Fiedler himself opened the door to his office. The light from the room temporarily flooded the darkened hall, as he guided me in. While shaking my hand he said, "Miss Jones, welcome, I'm very glad to meet you." "And I, you!" I answered. "Thank you for arranging this audition and for the joy I know I'll feel, getting a chance to sing with the Boston Pops."

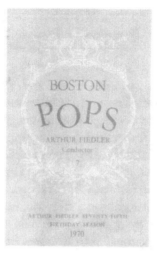

**Boston Pops Advertisement (1970)**

For his age, he was an amazingly handsome man; trim, elegant, and white haired with a mustache to match. "May I have the arias you're planning to sing?" he asked. I handed them to him. While he perused them, sitting at his shiny black grand piano, I had the opportunity to look around the room. A shelf three quarters of the way up the wall ran around the entire circumference of the room. On this shelf I was fascinated to find firemen's hats placed end to end. Below the shelf were framed shots of Fiedler conducting famous artists as they performed with the Orchestra. Incidentally, one of the eye-catching shots appeared in the program on the night of my performance. On the wall I saw the Maestro sitting in what appeared to be an antique fire engine. He was wearing a white fireman's hat and a duster to match. Beneath the picture was printed, "Mr. Fiedler and his own fire engine, outside Symphony Hall"

He called me to the piano. This brought me out of my silent

reverie.  An approving smile crept across his face as I sang the first few phrases of Liu's aria "Tu che di gel sei cinta" from Puccini's last opera, _Turandot_.  Liu is in love with the Prince, who in turn is in love with the icy Princess Turandot. In the aria, she warns Turandot, "You will melt and warm to the Prince's passion, but no matter how much you torture me, I shall never reveal his name, because once his name is known according to your previously stated command, the Prince will be beheaded.  The day has arrived when I shall close my eyes forever, keeping his name secret, though, sadly we shall never be together and I will see his face no more."  After Liu makes her pitiful plight known, she grabs a dagger from a nearby soldier and stabs herself, falling dead at the feet of the newly arrived Prince.

The Maestro commented favorably about my singing of this aria and said he was anxious to hear what I would do with the second piece.  I had chosen "My Man's Gone Now," from Gershwin's _Porgy and Bess,_ a bluesy lament, both sung and wailed, by the character Serena.  She stands, leaning over her murdered husband's dead body as it lies at her feet, and sobbingly sings:

> "....My man's gone now,
> ain't no use of listening,
> for his tired footsteps,
> climbin' up de stairs...."

After the last chord of the second aria, Fiedler rose to his feet and came around the piano with his arms extended.  His critique truly warmed my heart.  "You sing them both convincingly well.  I'm looking forward to the performance. The audience has a real treat in store for them."

A rehearsal with the orchestra before the concert is an absolute necessity.  Where exactly do I stand on stage?  If I stand too far forward, I cannot see the conductor.  If I stand too far back (being so tall), neither maestro nor the first violinist (concertmaster), are able to see each other. Their doing so is of paramount importance. Experience has taught me that, relying on my valuable peripheral vision, I can communicate freely with the audience while still able to follow the conductor's direction. During rehearsal, Fiedler physically choreographed the music like a dancer, so that the soloist and orchestra would perform as a cohesively, rhythmic entity. I was sure the audience would be enchanted by his translation of the music into multi-dimensional movements.

Finally, the much anticipated night of the concert arrived. In a hotel room near Symphony Hall, I went through the usual pre-concert rituals of preparing myself for a performance. Singing is an aerobic endeavor. It is essential that I have exercised daily beforehand, so that my body is strong, well coordinated and can in an instant do my bidding. In case I do not have access to a piano, I always carry a pitch pipe with me. This helps as I warm up the voice. Heaven forbid that my sound should, somehow, become a nuisance to the other guests. I generally check out the bathroom's exhaust system as soon as I arrive. It can carry the voice between the rooms. Many times I have had to tune up inside a darkened closet with the doors shut tight so as not to disturb anyone.

After gently putting my voice through its paces, I silently applied heavier makeup for the stage, so the audience would be able to easily see my eyes, brows and mouth at a distance. I put on the pale green gown, with sparkling trimming around the scooped neckline, that I would wear for the performance and did my hair, spraying it to stay in place.

Every pre-concert machination is an individual piece of a puzzle. When all the pieces are in place, one senses an unbelievably strong unified entity, to be used as a springboard in the production of a beautiful sound while simultaneously one retains the drama inherent within the character one is portraying. I wanted Liu to sound as Puccini envisioned her.

On June 8, 1970, at Boston's Historic Symphony Hall, the orchestra opened the concert with a march from _The Damnation of Faust_ by Berlioz and then played the "Academic Festival Overture" by Brahms. What an appropriate choice. After the applause died down, it was my turn to make my entrance. Arthur Fiedler momentarily walked offstage towards where I waited in the wings. He took my hand and led me onstage to the exact spot where I was to stand and sing. As I passed by, the orchestra members acknowledged me with a smile, a nod, and gently tapping on their instruments. The Maestro stepped up on the podium, picked up his baton and held it aloft for a few seconds to get everyone's attention. He then gave the musicians a decisive downbeat and they began the fragile introduction to my first aria. The beauty of their sound enveloped me, bearing me aloft. As I began to sing Liu's aria, with its oriental flavor, I felt a sweet shift in consciousness. My carefully assembled technique served as the springboard I imagined, allowing me to experience the flow state with which runners and other athletes are familiar. I felt as though my voice was a surfer riding the exhilarating crests of the swells and also the calm of the troughs, all the while being supported by symphonic ocean waves. After the aria, I smiled and mimed "Thank you" with my lips, as I bowed and acknowledged the audience's animated applause.

An anticipatory quiet settled over the hall, as the orchestra and I both prepared ourselves, technically and emotionally, for the last aria, "My Man's Gone Now." Following Fiedler's lead, the music took on the rhythmic, heart wrenching aura that the title implies. Gershwin was a past master at composing the classical jazz-opera that everyone has grown to love and understand. At the end, as I sang the last of Serena's wails, extending an octave and a half into the stratosphere and back down, some of the audience sprang to their feet applauding while others joined in enthusiastically from their seats. Fiedler stepped down from the podium and embraced me, whispering, "Wonderful!" into my ear. I was filled with the dizzying joy of success.

## PICTURES AFTER THE PERFORMANCE:

Directly after a wedding, the bride and groom generally delay their much awaited entrance at the reception in order to have formal pictures taken. So it was that before meeting the public after my performance with the Boston Pops, the Maestro, looking spiffy in his white tux and I in my green gown, prepared to pose. The photographer focused his camera until he was satisfied. Between Fiedler and me, however, there was quite a large height disparity. I immediately took off my high heel shoes but I still towered over him. Seeing the difference, Fiedler said to the photographer, "Wait till I can get my balance, then shoot." Precariously balancing on his tip toes, he finally centered himself and held still long enough for one picture to be taken, only to have to repeat the "on toes" teeter totter with each successive photo. My college classmate, Marcia Zonis, joined in and made it an "in color" threesome. She and I both will always cherish forever the enclosed picture and memories of that evening.

**Boston Pops - Soloist With Arthur Fiedler (1970)**

# Initial Opera Experiences

## OPERA THEATER FOR CHILDREN:

When my accompanist, Don Comrie, was not playing for me or musically enhancing a service at Wilton's Christian Science Church, he enjoyed accompanying many other diversified musical groups. If he found that he could incorporate my particular talent into these events, he did so without hesitation. One of these groups was the New Haven Opera Society and its "Opera Theater for Children," which performed at the Yale University Theater.

They were scheduled to perform both Rossini's *Cinderella* and Ashley Vernon's *The Triumph of Punch*. Don found a small part for me in *Triumph of Punch*, the role of Elisetta, which was miniscule. In fact I think I only had one sentence to sing in the entire opera. Being in this production, however, afforded me a bountiful beginning. It was the first time I was able to meet, sing, and work with other serious hopefuls on the very brink of their professional careers. One such person was Abraham Lind-Oquendo from Puerto Rico, who became a lifelong friend and colleague. Over time we were to sing many a duet from *Porgy and Bess* locally and also star in Opera/South's production of Beethoven's *Fidelio* in Jackson, Mississippi. Abe went on to have a career both in Germany and Israel and sang the role of Porgy in a Broadway production of *Porgy and Bess.* Other "Opera Theater for Children" cast members who had substantial opera careers include Susan Daveny Wyner, Cynthia Munzer, and Richard McKee.

## METROPOLITAN OPERA STUDIO:

The grant I received from the Metropolitan Opera to study voice, opened many new doors for me. Because of it, I was welcomed as an official member of the Metropolitan Opera Studio, whose main purpose was to groom and give experience to young talented artists with outstanding voices.

Five people from the Studio were subsequently given the opportunity to sing at a Lecture-Tea sponsored by the Metropolitan Opera Guild at New York's chic Colony Club. There were two baritones, two mezzos and one tenor. I was the only soprano. We sang excerpts from Wagner's _Das Rheingold._ It was only a reading of the score, so we were not fully staged. George Schick, a maestro at the Met, worked with us both individually and in ensembles. I sang the role of Woglinde, one of the swimming Rheinmaidens guarding the Rheingold. Wagner's music conjured up images of bubbling, shimmering clear water. I had no idea I would find myself in costume on stage singing this same role in a complete production accompanied by symphony orchestra. I was fortunate to have had this early chance to sing it in an unpressured performance with the Metropolitan Opera Studio.

## BORIS GOLDOVSKY'S OPERA WORKSHOP:

In the days before television, If one happened to turn on the radio on a Saturday afternoon, one would hear a familiar voice saying, "Good afternoon ladies and gentlemen, this is Milton Cross broadcasting live from the Metropolitan Opera House in New York City." Along with the ever present, "Texaco Opera Quiz," a popular intermission feature was "Opera News on the Air" with Boris Goldovsky. During this segment of the broadcast, Goldovsky analyzed the opera, and in an illuminating and entertaining way played excerpts on the piano. Besides heading his own opera company in Boston, he also each summer ran a successful Opera Workshop in Wheeling, West Virginia.

Don Comrie knew Boris Goldovsky through his connection with The Manhattan School of Music and strongly recommended that I audition and possibly attend Goldovsky's West Virginia Workshop. Comrie felt that the experience I would gain would be invaluable as I moved closer to a career in opera. Thanks to a successful audition, I was accepted into the Workshop. This meant I had to be away from home four whole weeks. I had no idea how Doug would feel about this, since he would have the full responsibility for the care and feeding of Jeff and Janet, ages 14 and 12. I broached the subject timorously. A warm compassionate smile, in reaction to my query, radiated from Doug's face as he gently said, "Sweetie Pie, what a wonderful opportunity for you to grow and learn! I'll come down to Wheeling to hear your performance. Don't worry about me and the children. We'll hold the fort until you come home".

My Workshop destination in West Virginia was a State College Dormitory where we were to stay. Upon arrival, I was shown to my room. I had not been inside a college dormitory since my days at Sarah Lawrence College. Being there made me feel good inside, as if I was coming home after a long absence. The music chosen by Goldovsky for us to perform in the College's elegant auditorium was Johann Strauss's _Die Fledermaus._ Strauss was known for his light, charming, three beats to the measure music and was crowned "The Waltz King" of the age.

The story underscoring _Die Fledermaus_ ("The Bat") reminds one of opera plots that Mozart set to music, plots filled with mistaken identities, delicious denouements and attention capturing intrigue. _Die Fledermaus_ was borrowed from a French play considered to be a fetching, light farce. Boris Goldovsky's extensive knowledge of the involutions and convolutions of the plot was indispensable to its success. He helped us understand what each character was thinking at any given moment and how to perfect and integrate the music and the staging.

There was a surprise in store for me that I had not anticipated. It was exciting to be given the female starring role of Rosalinda to sing. What I had not bargained for was that I could only perform in Act 1. There were two other sopranos, who, much to their delight, Goldovsky had sing Act ll and Act lll, respectively. So there would not be any confusion before the curtain went up, the audience was told of the cast changes ahead of time.

When we cast members were not rehearsing, we would hang out with one another. On occasion, some of the State College students would invite us to their on-campus parties. Although drinking liquor was forbidden, we did secretly imbibe a little. If someone from the establishment came to the door, we were cautioned to hide our glasses as quickly as possible. One of the students sitting next to me asked a puzzling question. He inquired, "Do you know how to play moon got you?" I told him, "No." He then said, "Come outside with me and I'll show you." So, we went downstairs and walked along the sidewalk a bit. He motioned for me to join him sitting on a bench. Pointing up to the luminous moon shining in the starry night sky, he asked, "See the moon?" I said "Ah hah." He then reached over and gave me an innocent hug and laughingly blurted out, "Got-cha!" What a charming trick I fell for.

The students who entertained us that evening were so intrigued with our group of opera hopefuls that they all attended our opening night performance. Goldovsky's Workshop had prepared me well. I felt very secure singing the Act l duet, two trios and finale. My only costume was a dressing gown I just happened to have brought from home. It sufficed. The performance exceeded our expectations in every way possible, and the audience responded in kind.

There is always a tinge of nostalgic sadness accompanying a cast's farewells. We had bonded strongly with one another while rehearsing and performing, but now it was time to say goodbye, pack up, and return to the reality of everyday living. We learned a lot together and were all thankful for the excellent experience. Two of the artists I met at the 1969 Goldovsky Workshop went on to have major careers. They were mezzo Florence Quivar and pianist Richard Lalli.

**Rosalinda - "Die Fledermaus"**
Goldovsky Opera Workshop Wheeling, West Virginia (1969)

Many years later, when I was singing major roles at The New York City Opera, Boris Goldovsky asked me to participate in one of his Metropolitan Museum of Art Lecture Series. I learned and sang the difficult title role in Richard Strauss's _Salome._ Boris mentioned in his introduction that I had formerly been one of his West Virginia Workshop students and that he was proud of my many later accomplishments.

## BOSTON OPERA:
Singers' roles can be organized in a descending order of decreasing difficulty and importance. The most coveted are the leading or primary roles. Next are the secondary roles which are not as long but still demand some vocal and dramatic excellence. Below that are the comprimarios who have the easiest of the shorter roles. They may even change their costumes quickly after singing in a particular scene, only to return later and play an entirely different character.

Supernumeraries or extras do not sing or dance but simply lend their costumed presences to fill out the crowd scenes, enhancing them with their well rehearsed, believable pantomime. The singing chorus and dance corps are two other specialized group categories.

How does one manage to get a toe hold on the lowest rung of the ascending ladder to a successful operatic career? Luck and being in the right place at the right time had a big influence on my triumphs. As in "....six degrees of separation...," you do not have to look very far to find a person with good connections. At first you must act as your own agent. Tell everyone you know and meet what you have done musically, what you are about to do, and what you would like to be doing in the future. You set your own course and people are exceedingly happy to help you attain your goals.

Linda Cabot Black, a descendent of Boston's historic Cabot family and one of the founders of the Boston Opera Company, heard me sing in a *Messiah* performance at the Wilton Congregational Church. She immediately set up an audition for me to sing for Sarah Caldwell, Boston Opera's Artistic Director. This turned out to be the real turning point in my life. I auditioned in New York for her and a few days later I received a call from Caldwell herself, telling me that she would like to engage me to sing in her next production, *Louise* by Charpentier. "What part will I sing in it?" I asked. "The role of the ex-prostitute who has become a street singer and sweeper of horse droppings," she answered. Caldwell then added that I would also be given the part of the forewoman in a dressmaking establishment. I laughed to myself after I had accepted her offer and hung up. "Type casting!" I giggled. I was enjoying, in retrospect, the sassy silent humor of my inner closed circuit television in which I was the only performer and viewer. So, my first appearance on a nationally known opera stage was to be as a comprimario, quick change artist. At last I had managed to step onto one of the lower rungs of the ladder to success.

Where to stay? Doug's grandfather had lived and reared his family in Boston, so I was welcomed to stay with his Aunt Lillie and her husband Clem during my rehearsal and performance time.  It was gratifying to get to know his many uncles, aunts and cousins, who were all very spiritual, loved to sing, and were the color of elegant mahogany.  Instead of living alone in a hotel room after exhausting rehearsals, I luxuriated in the relaxing, protective bosom of the Jones family. Public transportation took me daily from Roxbury's black neighborhood to the theater.

Unknown to me before my arrival, Miss Caldwell had cautioned those of the cast who were present, "Joining us tomorrow is Betty Jones, a soprano from Wilton, Connecticut.  She is a wife and mother, so this is perhaps her first time on the professional opera stage.  Be kind, gentle and supportive of this talented opera novice with such a beautiful voice." They all compassionately followed her advice, thank goodness!

My first _Louise_ rehearsal was in a most unusual setting.  The building was called The Cyclorama Hall Rotunda, a place that until recently had been a flower market.  It had a 129-foot skylight dome and was second in size only to a similar one in Washington, DC. The huge circular area was used to create an impression of a section  of Montmartre in Paris.  Set painters had brought to life blue sky, green trees and an unpaved street leading off into infinity, while carpenters had constructed a two-storied interior view building, completing the illusion of a dressmaking establishment where I was to be the forewoman.

The opening night of the opera had been postponed many times because  Boston City officials felt that the old building did not meet fire and safety requirements and should be condemned.  Somehow Sarah Caldwell got wind of when the influential safety inspectors were to arrive for a final review. Carol Neblett, soprano, was to sing the leading role of Louise, recreating her recent great success at the New York City Opera. Her on-stage lover, John Alexander, tenor, sang the role of Julien. They and the whole cast, after weeks of rehearsals, were flawlessly prepared. On a given cue from Caldwell, we presented our newly perfected, beguilingly beautiful music when the inspectors first arrived. It was hoped that our touching performance would tip the balance of good fortune in our favor. Carol Neblett, as Louise, sang her difficult love aria "Depuis le jour" with great ease, spinning high notes quietly at the very top of her range. The following Friday, with fire inspection documents and building permit in hand, the ingenious Sarah Caldwell's Boston Opera Company was allowed to premiere _Louise_ in a legally proclaimed safe building. One problem solved --- a few more to go.

Numerous night people, including rag pickers, inhabited the Montmartre Street scene. Their costumes were appropriately tattered and shabby. On one break between acts, a number of them decided to make it a coffee break. They left the theater for only a few moments, returning to find police blocking their re-entry. The police had confused the performers, because of their appearance, with the local bums and beggars in the area. The men in blue withdrew in embarrassment when they learned the truth about their mistaken identities. Also, how was Sarah Caldwell to know that the building she had carefully chosen to become her theatrical home was situated across the street from a busy police station? At any given moment during a performance, a police car's siren would wail loudly, signaling its departure and drowning out the music being sung and played on stage.

My props for the show consisted of a red feather boa and a broom for use by the ex-prostitute turned street sweeper. For my other role as the forewoman in the dressmaking establishment, my props were a needle, pins, scissors and a tape measure. In addition, I was called to impersonate a statue in the park. For this role, I was directed to, in a white leotard, silently and motionless appear on a pedestal.

One night as I slept, a dream warned me of an impending onstage disaster during the rehearsal of the sewing shop scene. The next day I was singing the role of the forewoman and was responsible for fitting and pinning dresses while others in the shop sewed them. The second floor room of the building, open to the audience, was a flurry of activity. All of a sudden, the entire set began to sway in reaction. Remembering my dream I was prompted to yell, "Everybody off the stage! The building's going to collapse!" All heads swiveled toward me and eyes and mouths sprang open wide. Gingerly, we all tip-toed down to stage level and in unison heaved a sigh of safe and sound relief. Carpenters and other backstage personnel rushed on to the set with hammer and nails in hand, to shore up this dangerously rickety structure.

I doubt that ever in the history of show business has there been a cast who prayed more assiduously for clear skies on performance nights. We knew that the patrons who paid the most for their tickets were to be seated down front nearest the stage. We also knew that in the event of rain, these same patrons, seated underneath the large glass dome, would be subjected to a disconcertingly cruel Chinese torture. The old building's roof would begin to leak directly over them.

On opening night under a clear sky, over 1,600 opera lovers, packed closely together, filled the auditorium. Their jubilantly reactive applause for what they saw and heard was deafening. Reviews in the Boston Globe and other newspapers the next day were long and ecstatic. Although I had very little to sing as a comprimario, nevertheless, I was still singled out, highlighted and given a much appreciated accolade in print and, at the ripe old age of 41, a boost to the next ladder rung of success.

## CHICAGO LYRIC OPERA COMPANY:

I reached the next rung when, without my ever having to audition, the Chicago Lyric Opera Company offered me the opportunity to sing in Richard Strauss's, _Der Rosenkavalier_. My role, a secondary one, was that of Marianne Leitmetzerin, duenna to the young and attractive Sophie.     The cast included Christa Ludwig as The Marschalin, Judith Blegen, who was also making her Chicago Lyric Opera debut, as Sophie, Charlotte Berthold sang the role of Octavian and Hans Sotin, Baron Ochs.

When the curtain goes up after the overture, the audience is treated to a beautiful boudoir scene in 18th Century Vienna. The bedroom is festooned with diaphanous, shimmering curtains.  In the middle of the stage, in a king size bed, two lovers relax after a frolicsome night of passionate love making. They are the Marschalin, a mature woman, and Octavian, a Count but  a  youth of only 17. When Mohammed, the Marshalin's page, brings her breakfast, Octavian scurries away and hides, returning only when all is quiet again. The Marschalin confides in Octavian that she has had an upsetting dream about her husband the night before.

A disturbance outside the door quickly returns her to reality. She is panic stricken, fearing that her husband has returned unexpectedly.   Octavian disappears, once again, this time returning disguised as the serving maid, Mariandel.  (The opera plot reminds one of Mozart's _The Marriage of Figaro,_ as it centers on the antics of aristocrats and royalty and, like _Figaro,_ is  based on a farcical comedic model of French origin.) The Marschalin, afraid her dalliance will be discovered, opens the bedroom door to find out what all the commotion is about.  She is relieved to find that it is the arrival of her cousin, Baron Ochs. Ochs has come to say that he is planning to get married and has chosen the well connected Sophie to become his wife. Sophie would also like to marry but has no idea that this bulbous bellied, reprehensible oaf is planning to ask her.  It is the local custom to have a silver rose presented to one's intended as an official sign of engagement and intention to marry. Ochs asks the Marschalin if she can suggest someone to accomplish this formality. She thinks a moment, then answers Octavian, a stranger to Ochs. Octavian has been standing close by listening but is still disguised as the young girl, Mariandel. Later, the Baron takes a shine to her and much to Octavian's disgust, flirts outrageously.

The duenna, my role, is not seen or heard by the audience until Act ll, when Octavian, now handsomely dressed all in silver, prepares to present the perfumed silver rose to Sophie as planned. The instant attraction between Sophie and Octavian is immediately evident to all present. As the Baron waits for the formality to be completed, he gets drunk on the celebratory wine. Sophie is instantly repulsed by his manner and appearance. To make matters worse, Ochs lustily chases the serving girls from room to room, leaving Octavian and Sophie by themselves. Alone together at last, they exchange kisses. Sophie swears she will never marry Ochs, and Octavian promises to love and protect her forever. The Baron returns and tries to strong arm Sophie into signing the marriage contract. Octavian intervenes by unsheathing his sword and draws a little of Ochs's blood as a warning to desist. The Baron wails and groans as though he has been mortally wounded.

At the end of the opera, the Marschalin returns to the scene and puts an end to the tumult by insisting that the Baron leave forthwith. All ends well when Octavian and Sophie are finally free to explore each other in depth.

Richard Strauss's music is so achingly beautiful that I never missed not singing any of the solo arias. There were many duets, trios, and quartets in which we were joined by other voices that tested our artistic know-how and vocal technique. Dramatically, the duenna supports her charge, Sophie, emotionally. In every way I know I projected this on stage.

The costumes were beautifully appliqued with bows, sparkles, and voluminous lace. All the women of class wore hooped skirts in the form and style worn during the reign of Austria's Maria Theresia. As in The *Marriage of Figaro,* the characters in *Der Rosenkavalier* succeed in plots to discredit the veracity of the lead philandering male and truth triumphs in the end.

"Der Rosenkavalier" - Chicago Lyric Opera (1973)

# Additional Performances and Getting a Manager

After my professional opera debut in Boston at the age of 41 on March 12 1971, the following year turned out to be a banner one in the development of my budding career. In February I did my second New York recital to a sold-out house at Lincoln Center's Alice Tully Hall. Peter Davis of the New York Times wrote on February 14th, 1972, "MISS JONES, SOPRANO DISPLAYS FINE VOICE." He continued:

> "....From a purely vocal standpoint, Betty Jones's Tully Hall recital Sunday afternoon was outstanding. Her soprano is a rich and full bodied instrument that moves with easy assurance throughout its compass. The top rings out clearly---only a hint of a fluttery vibrato intrudes, a touch of intriguing individuality rather than a flaw in this case---and her lower range has the strength and dark timbre that a mezzo might envy...."

Over the next several months, I was the soloist with the Buffalo Philharmonic Orchestra at the famous Eero Saarinen designed Kleinhans Music Hall in Buffalo, New York and made my first appearance with the Jacksonville Symphony in Florida. I later returned to sing in Jacksonville on many occasions, one of them when the Symphony was engaged to play for the opening game of the newly formed World Football League in 1974. This appearance was televised nationwide. Other 1972 engagements included the Johnstown Symphony Orchestra in Pennsylvania and the Ridgefield Symphony in Connecticut. In addition, I gave my first Candlelight Concert at the Wilton Congregational Church and one at Fairfield University.

Opening Night - World Football League
Jacksonville Symphony
Gator Bowl, Florida (1974)

## GETTING A MANAGER:

Up until then, most of my bookings were obtained through recommendations of influential friends. For example, the head of Triad Presentations, an organization to promote opportunities for black performers, which sponsored my Alice Tully Hall Concert, was a close friend of my parents and had known me since birth. Studying with coaches who are well connected can lead to lucrative singing engagements, but only a manager can provide the overall guidance needed to build a career in opera. A good manager is in touch with the world-wide music scene, can set up auditions and smooth the path ahead. I had auditioned for a couple of potential managers, but none seemed ready to take on an unknown inexperienced soprano. While, however, singing with the Boston Opera Company, I became friendly with many successful singers who were all under management. Based on my innate performing skills, one of the singers, a tenor, strongly advised me to call his manager, Hans J. Hofmann, and sing for him. "I'll bet he'll take you on," he added.

To my surprise, Hofmann agreed to hear me. I prepared myself well for the audition in hopes of making an impact on this dapper older man. I chose selections that would allow me to put on an impressive performance with all the attendant musical and dramatic bells and whistles. Adhering to the usual protocol, he asked me, "What would you like to sing?" I told him and sang it. Then he asked, "What else have you brought?" I told him the other three arias I had with me. From these he chose the one he would like to hear. The first aria always relaxes the singer. In an audition, pieces after that are selected to reveal both the singer's strengths and weaknesses. When Hofmann had heard enough to decide whether to represent me or not, he seriously scrutinized me and wanted to know more about me. "Thank you," he said, "that was really quite good." He continued more hesitantly, "There's a certain something about you ---." Deciding to help him out of his predicament I offered, "I'm of mixed heritage, I'm part black." He smiled, "That's it! That's it!" and spontaneously clasped his hands together. Afraid that he had perhaps upset me, he decided to placate me by offering, "That's all right. Don't worry about a thing. I'm Jewish! I just knew there was something different about you." In the future, engagement by engagement and brick by brick, Hofmann and I would work together amicably to build my career from the bottom up.

# Wagner's Ring with San Francisco Opera

The highlight of San Francisco Opera's 50th Anniversary was Richard Wagner's four opera epic _Der Ring Des Nibelungen_, the longest and most complex work in the history of all opera. Three complete cycles of the _Ring_ were scheduled to be performed during San Francisco's 1972 fall season.

Luckily, I had the good fortune to have worked with Otto Guth, an influential coach, when preparing for my _Das Rheingold_ performance with the Metropolitan Opera Studio. As we perfected the role of Woglinde together, Guth was so taken with my voice that he called his friend, Kurt Herbert Adler, the General Director of the San Francisco Opera, to tell him of my seemingly limitless vocal range and talent for the German operatic repertoire. A short time later, I was thrilled to be asked to audition for the San Francisco Opera and was engaged on the spot to sing in three of the four planned Ring operas. They included the roles of Woglinde in _Das Rheingold,_ Gerhilde in _Die Walküre_ and Woglinde, again, in _Götterdämerung._ I considered Gerhilde to be the most difficult of the three; in fact, I almost fainted when I became aware of how many high notes were demanded by the role. The music was filled with beautiful but declamatory bombast. My voice had to be heard over an entire symphony orchestra playing at top volume.

How does one prepare physically for the rigors of convincingly portraying a role in Wagner's Ring Cycle? One trains like an Olympic athlete, that is how! Our daughter Janet studied dance with Bambi Lynn, a Broadway dancer who had a studio in Westport, Connecticut. Her husband, Joe DeJesus, taught exercise classes and took me on as a special student. I learned from him how to strengthen and limber up my body through weight lifting, endurance and stretching exercises. Fortified by this specialized training, I was easily able to meet the demands expected of me when I arrived in San Francisco for my first rehearsal.

Drawing from Norse mythology, Wagner used a different dramatic plot for each opera. The operas deal with three earth realms: beneath the surface where the Nibelung Dwarfs live, the surface of the earth inhabited by giants as well as ordinary mortals, and the cloudy heights that are the home of the Gods. The stories of these four operas expose a panoply of human like failings, from the most base to the transcendent, from duplicity, murder, lust and incest, to the self effacing heroic strengths of courage, love and caring. A list of colorful characters run the gamut of Gods, Goddesses, Giants, Dwarfs, and Rhine-daughters. Mix in some magic with the brilliance of Wagner's music and one has the elements in place to entertain and fascinate the world.

## DAS RHEINGOLD:

As Woglinde in the lyric, rippling music of _Das Rheingold_, I sang the role of one of a trio of frolicsome water nymph sisters swimming beneath the surface of the Rhine River. The Rhinemaidens main responsibility is to protect the magic gold from thieves. It glitters and glimmers like a tantalizing underwater beacon, from the top of a two-story tall rock formation the Rhinemaidens swim in and out of. Whoever, through subterfuge, gains the gold can melt it down, fashion a ring and, through its magic, gain the power to rule the entire world.

We were told that as important as the hours of preparatory music rehearsals, was learning how to commando crawl. I had no notion why we had to perfect that type of locomotion, but it was said to be a top priority. Daily, we three Rhinemaidens, Gwen Jones, Sandra Walker and Betty Jones were driven to a local State Armory to be shown the maneuvers and practice. On the first day, as we arrived, we saw National Guard soldiers in uniform energetically marching in perfect cadence. They were dumbfounded when we three seemingly elegant ladies were directed to get down, belly flat on the floor and slowly snake slither our way across the room. I was sure the stage director and his assistant knew what *Das Rheingold* demanded, even if I did not understand their requests. I just kept my mouth shut and did what they told me to do, to the best of my ability.

Rehearsals in their early phase usually took place in a room with a piano. As the performance began to take form, it was moved on stage. The time then came for us to learn, as quickly as possible, how to scale the inner hollow heights of the on-stage rock formation and sing out of designated openings between the mock rocks.

During the first scene, a transparent curtain called a scrim is stretched across the entire stage front. It serves as a screen through which underwater light images emanating from a rear projection booth can shine, while not obscuring the Rhinemaidens and the rock which is their home. The first time that I climbed up on the inside of the rock formation and stuck my sleek, scaled body out of its rugged window to sing in close harmony with my fish sisters, "Weia! Waga! Woge du Wella," a spear of fright pierced my consciousness. I became aware, for the first time, how high in the air I was. It was a dizzying realization! The top balcony of the opera house and I were on the same level. This was one of those rare times when I had to firmly put my trepidations behind me and live entirely in the character of Woglinde. I had to think what she would have been thinking at the time. I then became free to actually become a Rhinemaiden without any extraneous thoughts and fears. Woglinde's essence won the battle against my temerity!

We Rhinemaidens decided that the Rhine River must flow from right to left. I choreographed the breast stroke while swimming to the right, upstream against the current, and then resting while floating left, downstream again, with a minimum of movement. As the scene progressed, the large scrim was raised. In front of it was a three-foot tall smaller one, behind which we could enter and exit the stage at the beginning and end of our scene. At last we were called upon to use our much touted commando crawl in order to be completely hidden from the audience.

Our beautiful dark blue-green costumes, leotard and tights, were covered with hand painted fish scales highlighted in gold. The sculpted bathing caps looked like three dimensional hair locks, shimmering in reflective light to match the rest of our mermaid costumes. Make-up artists emphasized the contours of our faces by applying gold makeup to our cheek bones, chins, brows and noses.

**"Das Rheingold"**
(with G. Jones, S. Walker, B. Jones & Coach Otto Guth
San Francisco Opera (1972)

After the opening overture, the first act's action revolves around the guarding of the magic gold by the swimming sisters, Woglinde, Wellgunde and Flosshilde, and the arrival of the lecherous, dangerous dwarf Alberich. His one purpose is to steal the gold and thereby reign over all with its unleashed hidden powers. He tries to climb nearer the top of the rock but sings about the rock's inaccessibility, "loathsome, slimy, slippery pebble!" He berates it, "I cannot stand! My hands and feet can't hold on to your treacherous smoothness." He then decides to try to woo each maiden in turn, enticing them to leave the gold unguarded and swim down to his level. Alberich continues, "Fling your slender arms around me so I can stroke you and toy with your beautiful tresses." This request is directed to the Rhinemaiden Wellgunde. She is not amused and takes immediate offense. Indignantly, she answers, "Be gone you hairy, hideous, swarthy, sulfurous smelling dwarf! Go find some other sweetheart whom you can perhaps please, for I can't stand you!" Eventually Alberich catches the maidens off guard and undaunted, scampers up to the top of the rock, steals the coveted gold from its peak and quickly disappears into the thickening darkness, its three guardians in hot pursuit, singing woefully, "Help us! Help us! -- Help."

## DIE WALKÜRE:

The next opera in the Ring Cycle, _Die Walküre,_ also tested my stamina and ingenuity. "Die Walküre" is German for the English "The Valkyries." There are nine Valkyries, warrior maiden daughters of the reigning God, Wotan. They honor and obey their father's directive to pick up those men who have died gloriously on the battlefield and carry them on their horses to Valhalla. The legendary soprano Birgit Nilsson, who I worshipped, sang the demanding role of Brünnhilde.

There were, of course, no real horses on stage. Nine horses at once? Can you imagine what confusion their presence would have caused? Before being seen by the audience, each sister in turn made believe that she had just dismounted in the wings before her entrance.

**"Die Walküre"**
**Washington Opera - Kennedy Center (1974)**

At the beginning of the third act, as Gerhilde, I was the first Valkyrie to breathlessly arrive at our predetermined gathering place near the woods. In the overture to Act III, the orchestra previewed our arrival by playing the well known "Ride of the Valkyries," a rhythmic horse galloping, war like music. I had studied and restudied the repetitive theme of this musical passage so that, in time to sing, I could run on stage precisely at the right moment. Somehow I would always get confused as to just when to make my entrance, so I elicited the help of an off-stage prompter. As the music unfurled, I nervously asked her, "Now?" She replied, "No -- no." I waited, then queried again, "Now?" The music continued a few more beats when she stage whispered to me, "OK -- Now!" Dressed in a full suit of metallic looking protective armor, a cape and a horned helmet, I rushed on stage. To complete the warrior look, I carried a five foot long spear in one hand and an oval full body shield in the other. The pointed tip of the spear was a lot heavier than the other end. Foreseeing a possible problem, the head prop man weighted the other end of the spear, too. Before every performance, I would search out the fulcrum of the spear, so that it balanced, and grasp it only at that place. After numerous rehearsals and three performances of wielding this cumbersome object, my biceps really began to bulge in an unfeminine manner. Emerging into the bright stage lights from the dark wings I, as Gerhilde, was the first on stage singing a rallying cry for my other sisters to hurry and join me, "Ho-yo-to-ho! Ho-yo-to-ho!" My cry climbed higher and higher, increasing the musical tension as it went up the scale.

On another occasion, when I sang *Die Walküre* with The Washington Opera Company in the National Capitol's Kennedy Center, I took the role of another sister, Ortlinde. In the same third act section, the melody continued rising even further until I reached and sang a high C while given needed encouragement by the support of the orchestra. The well known bass George London was our stage director for this particular production. When he first worked with us, he was impressed by how tall and strong we looked as a Valkyrie ensemble. He compared our performance with that of an Italian tenor singing in a concert many years earlier. He then confided to the Washington Valkyrie sisters, "Every piece the tenor sang was equally as loud as every other. I knew there must be quiet sections indicated by the composer here and there." London said that after the performance he went backstage to greet the tenor. He complimented him on his beautiful voice adding, "I think your performance could have benefitted from a few delicate dynamic shadings." The tenor inflated his chest like a peacock and replied in his thick italian accent, "When-a-you got-it,---you-a show it off!"

After one of our long and exhausting rehearsals, the nine Valkyrie sisters decided to have dinner together at one of Washington, DC's popular restaurants. The maitre d' who greeted us at the door was visibly shaken when he saw how tall and imposing we were. He brought the owner over and whispered, "But where can they sit? It's so over-crowded here already." His boss sizing up the situation chuckled as he replied: "Let 'em sit -- anywhere they WANT!"

"Die Walküre"
Valkyrie Sisters with Conductor Antal Dorati & Director George London
Washington Opera - Kennedy Center (1974)

## GÖTTERDÄMERUNG:

In the last opera of Wagner's epic Ring Cycle, _Götterdämerung_, the "Twilight of the Gods," I sang the role of Woglinde, one of the three Rhinemaidens who also appeared in the first opera, _Das Rheingold._ After an orchestral prelude at the beginning of the third act, the curtain rises revealing a woody, wild, rocky valley on the Rhine River. The river flows past a steep cliff in the background. The fish-like Rhinemaidens, Woglinde, Wellgunde, and Flosshilde, rise to the surface, behind a small scrim, and swim about, Esther Williams style, as if dancing. They sing, asking the sun to send its brilliant rays into the water. Up until then the river is dark like eternal night, without the magic gold to mirror its rays. When the Rhinemaidens sing about the darkness below, the melody and harmonies are written in a sad minor scale. The music returns to a happier major scale as they remember the past, when through the waves the radiant sunbeams are reflected by the Rheingold. "How bright was your luster, oh beauteous star of the water," they sing.

A famous horn solo sequence signals the imminent arrival of Siegfried, who appears on the cliff high above and is fully armed. The Rhinemaidens quickly realize that he is wearing the magic ring made from the stolen rheingold. They call to him by name in harmony, "Siegfried! --- Siegfried!" Woglinde teasingly asks him to return the ring. He agrees at first but then reconsiders and refuses. They warn him of the ill fate that will surely assail him because of its continued possession. They beg in song, "Give it back to us and you will be free forever of the ring's inherent curse." Feeling that they have failed in their attempt to repossess it, they sadly sink back down into the waves. Echoes of their themes are heard farther and farther in the distance as they swim away into total silence.

Then violence erupts; Siegfried is stabbed to death. Brünnhilde arrives and is horrified to find her beloved dead. She orders that a funeral pyre be built. After gently taking the ring from Siegfried's finger, she makes sure his body is placed with dignified honor on top of the logs. When the yellow flames rise high enough to obscure Siegfried's body, Brünnhilde sings her final aria, the most difficult in all of opera history. It goes on for almost 20 pages. Then, calling for her horse Grane, Brünnhilde sacrifices herself by riding directly into the thick of the flames, where she joyfully joins Siegfried in death's eternal bliss. The Rhine River overflows its banks in reaction and the Rhinemaidens rise to the surface again in the hopes of retrieving their ring.

In single file, as directed, we then commando crawled once again under the cover of the small scrim toward the dark quiet of the offstage wing. As we reached the home stretch, Jess Thomas, who sang the role of Siegfried, added to the evening's excitement by bending down low and in a stage whisper cheered us on, "Come on girls, you can do it! You're almost at the finish line." One by one as we arrived off stage, Jess surprised the Rhinemaidens by sweeping us up in his arms, hugging and giving each in turn a kiss on the cheek. "You see, you made it!" he said, jubilantly under his breath, with a big warm smile, while pantomime clapping his hands together in total silence.

In retrospect, I was very happy not to be singing the role of Brünnhilde. When Birgit Nilsson sang the daunting "Immolation Scene" aria that ends *Götterdämerung*, even the Fire Marshal, who must be present on-stage at all times, watched and listened attentively. He was mesmerized whenever Nilsson sang. He has heard them all, but her brilliance temporarily made him suspend his usual blaze' boredom. She had to have possessed Tarzan's corrugated abs in order to support such a difficult, gut-busting role. At the end of the opera, the whole audience jumped to its feet, shouted, clapped and yelled its appreciation. I watched as Nilsson prepared to take her bows. One of the stage crew held the curtain open so that she could easily pass through into the spotlight. I was astounded to hear her singing coloratura bird tweets in the top of her range at this time. I asked her, "Why are you singing way up there now when you've just sung hours of Brünnhilde?" She smiled knowingly and answered, "I'm just tuning up my voice in order to put it to bed for the night."

Years after this initial encounter with Birgit Nilsson, she and I found ourselves under the same management, Eric Semon Associates Inc.

# First Leading Role

While I was singing with the San Francisco Opera in 1972, Richard Rodzinski, the assistant to the General Director, recommended me to Glynn Ross, the head of the Seattle Opera Company, as a possible "Aida." The company was planning a special production to celebrate the grand opening of a new civic center in Phoenix, Arizona. Ross and another member of his staff flew down from Seattle to hear me. I certainly did not know the entire role but luckily had studied one aria, Ritorna Vincitor (Return Victorious) from Act I. After singing it for them, ear to ear smiles was their reaction and later I was told that Ross was heard to say, "She's a little raw and awfully tall but --- she's certainly an Aida." Damn! Why did I wear those high heels anyway?

So I was engaged to sing my very first major operatic role. It was written into my contract, however, that I must report to Seattle on the day after my final performance of *Götterdämmerung.* Needless to say, I was excited about the chance to sing Aida but, after being in San Francisco for almost two months, I found that I was eagerly looking forward to returning to Wilton and seeing my husband and children. Our son, Jeff had been elected Wilton High School's first Homecoming King and Janet was missing her Mom most keenly while I was away. Even though Doug had made a couple of trips across the country to see and hear me, I really missed him and home. I called him on the telephone just to hear his voice and to relieve my lonesome longings. He said, "Sweetie Pie, we'll be together soon. I'll fly out to see you in your final performance and then accompany you to Seattle to help you get settled." I immediately felt better and cheerfully returned to my work.

Life has taught me that most things happen for the best. Earlier that year, my husband had been on a business trip to

Texas.   On the flight home he sat next to an interesting attorney with whom he found he had many interests in common.   Since Doug had parked his car at LaGuardia Airport, he offered on arrival to drop his fellow traveler off at his Westchester home while driving to Wilton.   When Doug mentioned that I was an aspiring opera singer, the attorney said, "I have a large box of opera tapes at home given me by one of my clients.   You can have any of the tapes you want with my best wishes and thanks." Doug chose *Aida* with Leontyne Price singing the title role.   Sometime later, as I was packing for the trip to sing the *Ring* in San Francisco, something told me to take along the *Aida* tape. What a phenomenal blessing its possession proved to be, since I had never studied the entire role with either an accompanist, or more importantly, a voice teacher.

Doug joined me in San Francisco as promised to hear my last performance of *Götterdämmerung.*   The next day, we flew together to Seattle, where he helped me move into my new living quarters.   I took up residence in an old hotel I had first heard about while singing in San Francisco. It was run by the Salvation Army and the price was miniscule.   The rooms were pleasant and clean, the linen was changed once a week and the residents were given one main meal a day in the dining room.   As the popular song goes,   "Who could ask for anything more?" The Salvation Army's employees truly lived the Christian ethic that their organization professes.   They were warm, helpful and very supportive of us all.   Women of every age and all walks of life lived there, including a young nun who had just left the order.   I heard that on occasion she entertained a gentleman in the communal living room.   Men were not allowed in the other rooms. Then I heard she was getting married. The entire hotel rejoiced over her   good fortune, and all of us were  invited to her wedding.

Because of this no male visitor rule, when my husband would visit me we  made arrangements to stay at a luxury hotel.   I enjoyed greatly the respite from my self imposed abstemious, penny pinching existence. I always aimed, whenever on the road, to take home as much of my pay as possible. Luckily, Doug had business projects and connections worldwide, so it became an absolute necessity that he check on engineering projects at the faraway places where I was performing.

I only had three and a half weeks in Seattle to perfect the role of Aida. The wonderful coaches and conductor took turns working with me around the clock. Besides being taught the staging and all the music in the scenes where I appeared, I had to know everyone else's music, because hidden in their melody or harmony might be the note I needed to hear to begin my next line. Opera had set before me a banquet of artistic disciplines to be conquered. It was up to me to ingest and fully digest them so that I could seem, in performance, to totally become Aida on stage.

My first big aria, "Ritorna Vincitor," which I already knew, is the more dramatic of the two big soprano arias in the score. The accompanying orchestration is fuller dynamically in all the vocal registers. "O Cieli Azzurri" (Oh Blue Skies), the second big aria, is lighter and more lyric. Verdi wrote a quiet, sustained killer high C for Aida to sing at the end of this aria. Up until shortly before my first performance, I could not sing the aria through, especially the last climactic note. Recognizing my problem during a coaching session, Conductor Henry Holt suggested, "Betty, you've got to make up your mind that you're going to sing it and then you will! Strong unswerving motivation will make it happen. You'll see!" Bless Leontyne Price for proving to me, on the wonderful tape I brought with me, that it is actually possible to sing the last high note with relaxed, gentle ease.

I think being of mixed racial lineage gave me special insight into Aida's dilemmas. In the opera, as Aida, I am an Ethiopian princess enslaved in Egypt and hand maiden to the Egyptian princess, Amneris. This is a story of conflicting loyalties and the triumph of love even unto death. Ethiopia

118

and Egypt are at war. Radames, the man I am secretly in love with and he with me, is also supreme commander of the Egyptian army. He is preparing to lead an attack against the Ethiopian forces led by Amonasro, the king of Ethiopia, my father. A crowd gathers to cheer Radames and his Egyptian forces on as they march by. I join in their patriotic demonstrative cheering which transforms musically into my first aria, "Ritorna Vincitor." Then rethinking my ecstatic outburst, I recant by singing, "How can I say such words so fraught with betrayal, to win the war against my father who only fought to free me from slavery and take me back to my own country, where by rights I can bear the exalted name of Princess?" Caught in such painfully opposing cross currents, my melodic themes shift accordingly, beginning with a joyful declamation, on to a pleading prayer that the Gods intervene and have pity, then to lyrically loving music about my beloved's tender passions, and ending with another intercession that the Gods end my sufferings forever.

As the plot unfolds, when asked, Radames innocently divulges to me secret information regarding the movements of the Egyptian forces. Because of this, he is branded as a traitor and is sentenced to death by asphyxiation in a sealed tomb. I slip into the tomb before he arrives so that I can be with him until the end, while Amneris paces above and begs pardon for facilitating this cruel judgment against the man she also loves. Entombed together, Radames and I sing a tragic duet. There are many stacatto notes (the shortest notes possible). I sing, "See, the death angel descend and heaven's portals open wide where pain and tears are ended! Soon we will wander side by side through love's enchanted door. Farewell earth --- oh vale of sorrow. In the stars we shall at last be free." While singing that part of the opera, I had the strangest feeling that I could smell incense burning within the tomb and that if I actually died, it would be all right.

How does one convincingly die on stage? Yes, you can lie very still but the audience can still see you breathing. With

119

input from my cousin Jane White, a professional actress, I taught myself to breathe on command with only my side ribs and not my upper chest or diaphragm. Friends, relatives and colleagues have greeted me after performances with the question, "We didn't see you breathe. We worried about you! How did you do it?"

Thanks to the tape I was given, the many rehearsals and Henry Holt's belief in me, I finally figured out how to produce that treacherous high C at the end of the Nile aria. It was then time for the whole cast and all the scenery to be transported from Seattle to Phoenix, Arizona for the long awaited much heralded opening of the new Civic Center. What a grand and glittering event it proved to be, with many important visitors, including President Nixon's daughter, Tricia, and the Governors of all 50 States. Arizona's Senator Barry Goldwater was the Honorary Chairman. Doug flew in from Connecticut to hear my performance. As the wise bromide states "All's well that ends well." The next day the Phoenix Gazette's review said of me:

> "....The title role was well portrayed by Betty Jones, a tall attractive soprano whose talents grew in powerful proportion to the opera's tragic tale of thwarted love and divided loyalties. It is the Nile Scene (Act III) that charms and Miss Jones stole it with lovely singing, sustained nicely throughout the tender finale (Oh earth farewell)...."

Since Aida was my first major role, I will be eternally indebted to Glynn Ross, Conductor Henry Holt and all the wonderful coaches at the Seattle Opera whose patience and faith in this unknown soprano added greatly to my success.

During my career, I sang many additional Aidas and other leading soprano roles in German and Italian. One of the Aidas I sang was, on returning to Seattle, a children's performance in English. It was evident from the beginning that the kids had all done their homework because they knew the plot and the musical themes. They surprised us all on the stage by loudly booing or cheering at appropriate intervals. When Radames and I sang our amorous duet, both he and I heard a strange sound emanating from the orchestra. We noted it, then shrugged it off and continued singing. Again the same sound distracted our attention. It sounded like the clink of metal hitting metal. When it happened a third time, the conductor, Henry Holt, with gathering furrowed brow, stopped the orchestra dead in its tracks, turned around to the audience and spoke out loudly, "The next kid who zings a paper clip down the bell of the base tuba ---- we'll stop the performance, close the curtain, pack up and all go home, so behave yourselves!"

**"Aida" - Seattle Opera - Denver (1975)**

# New York City Opera

My manager, Hans Hofmann must have heard via the music grapevine that the New York City Opera was looking for singers in certain vocal categories to perform hard-to-cast roles. My voice is classified as a "lyrico spinto" and therefore qualifies as unusual. It's a lyric voice that is malleable enough to be agile and able to sing coloratura and strong enough when not reined in to be heard over a full orchestra but when dramatic singing is called for, it is able to accomplish this desired effect. The word "spinto" comes from the Italian word "spingere," which means "to push." My nearly six foot height easily accomplishes these sounds which can be called for, on command, from my Steinway Concert Grand body. The longer the piano, the richer the sound.

Every leading singer in an opera company needs an understudy, or cover, to take over in case of illness. While the New York City Opera was trawling for new talent, I auditioned. After my manager reminded the City Opera officials that I had successfully sung the difficult role of Aida in Seattle and performed three complete cycles of Wagner's _Ring_ in San Francisco, I was called back for a second audition. Shortly afterwards, I received a call from Mr. Hofmann notifying me that I had been selected on the basis of my second audition to join the Company as a cover and, best of all, to sing major roles like Amelia in Verdi's _Un Ballo in Maschera,_ "A Masked Ball." As I listened on the phone to this exciting news, I could feel pleasurable pressure beginning to build within me like a suddenly active volcano ecstatically itching to spew forth lava into the high atmosphere. Determined to maintain my composure in spite of feeling otherwise, I answered questions, took notes and said a sane, "Thank you," then hung up after saying a polite, "Goodbye."

DAILY NEWS, SATURDAY, AUGUST 17, 1974

**Fresh Voices**

Betty Jones (L) and Catherine
Malfitano are among the nine
new singers and a conductor
and a stage director who will
make their debuts during the
City Opera's fall season, starting Aug. 28 at the State Theater with a performance of
Donizetti's "Lucia di Lammer-
moor" with Beverly Sills. The
new conductor is Frenchman
Michel Plasson. The new stage
director is Stephen Porter, artistic director of the New
Phoenix Repertory Co.

New York City Opera
Joining Announcement (1974)

I alleviated my psychological seismic build up by erupting into a shrill orgasmic scream of triumph as I streaked down the hall towards the bedroom to share with Doug all that had transpired on the phone. I giggled as I proudly told him, "Thanks to all your help, Doug, I've just been asked to sing the lead role of Amelia at Lincoln Center. Can you believe it?" We hugged, kissed and jumped up and down like two young children hearing long awaited good news. Doug immediately called to make a reservation for me at the Empire Hotel, directly across the street from the City Opera, while I packed. He then drove me to New York. Why the rush? He knew I needed to get comfortably acclimated to my new reality well in advance of the demands of starting rehearsals.

The appointed day arrived to begin rehearsals. I entered the New York State Theater at Lincoln Center through the stage door. When I read my name written on the rehearsal schedule, I sensed that I was ready for anything and everything, large or small. A confident, relaxed feeling washed over me when I was welcomed in so warmly and introduced to the coach who was to work with me that day. I knew right away that I was in good hands. He and I talked and got to know each other while taking my first guided tour of the building. One of the important things he brought to light was the fact that the New York City Opera's concert hall was not designed acoustically with musical events in mind, but meant for ballet instead. There was also no prompter's box down front center stage for a singer to rely on when the going gets tough and memory fails. In other opera houses, the prompter has a score to follow and a TV monitor's view of the conductor's movements to consult. From his well-lit box, he can point to the singer and mime the words just before each musical entrance. Yes, always secretly watch the conductor, but when in doubt, also check with the prompter. His only responsibility is the singer, not the orchestra. At the City Opera, without the convenience of the box, prompters are stationed in the wings on either side of the stage, making it difficult in the dark for them to transmit the intuitively sensed existence of impending problems or solve them before they happen and become known to the audience.

He also explained to me that singing in this theater lacked the encouraging rebound sound of the voice returning to the ear after it bounces off the walls of an acoustically well designed hall. The average person loves to sing in the shower or the car because he is in an enclosed space with hard walls and can really hear himself at his best. "Be careful not to oversing in performance and hurt yourself in your search for a more surround sound. The audience will hear you just fine although you might not think so," the coach said. As we walked down the hall to the rehearsal studio, I admitted, "I'm going to have to start from scratch. I've never studied Amelia, not even with my voice teacher, or performed any of _Ballo_ before." "That's all right," he replied encouragingly. "We've got enough time to work on it together until you feel totally secure in singing the role." As we reached the room reserved for us, I heaved a slow sigh of relief because I knew in my heart that he truly understood what needed to be done to make my New York debut as Amelia a success.

## UN BALLO IN MASCHERA:

Verdi based the story of _Un Ballo in Maschera_ on a tragic incident which actually happened in 1792, the assassination of King Gustav lll in Stockholm, Sweden. Regicide is a dangerously contagious and inflammatory act. Verdi changed the Swedish names to Italian so that he could set it in Italy, but the government censors would not hear of it. Finally Verdi set the opera in far away Boston, Massachusetts. The title of "King" was changed to that of "Governor" but, strangely, the Italian names were still left in tact. The Paris production of _Ballo_ in 1861 was set in Florence. A London performance was set in Naples. Ultimately, a completely uncensored Italian performance was set in Stockholm, where the murder of the king had actually taken place.

In the opera, Amelia has fallen in love with the targeted King Ricardo. As Amelia, I decide I must visit the lair of Ulrica, a sorceress, to enlist her assistance in helping me rid myself of my guilty yearning for Ricardo. I am married to Renato, the King's trusted confident. Unknown to Renato, Ricardo is equally enamored of me. Ricardo overhears Ulrica's proposed remedy, "that at midnight, pick a magic herb at the foot of the gallows," and he secretly vows to intercept me during my search for the plant.

As the next curtain rises, following Ulrica's instructions, I make my way to a desolate hill on the outskirts of town just before midnight. There, a foreboding silhouette of the execution gallows appears. As midnight approaches, I feel an icy fear grip my fast beating heart. I am wearing a white veil over my head in order to not be recognized. In semi-darkness, as the clock strikes twelve, I seem to see a whispy white apparition of a previously executed criminal rise from the ground. I sing in quivering terror, "He is glaring at me with a horrible stare." I am so confused and frightened that I sink to the ground and pray to God for help. "Lord in Heaven, oh hear my cry. Grant me thy mercy, Oh Father on high." My full length costume, of vintage style 1792, cushions

my knees as I kneel on the hard ground but makes it difficult
for me to quickly arise again on cue.  I am called upon by the
composer at this moment to sing a slow plaintive lament of
cascading notes, starting very high, well above the lines and
spaces of the score, then on down and finishing in the
mezzo sounding speaking range.

After my prayer, using all my might and main, I manage with
quasi grace to scramble to my feet and walk toward the tall
gallows to pick the plant.   A short orchestral interlude
suddenly picks up the rhythm.   The audience responds
emotionally to the mounting tension of ever rising higher
notes.   Ricardo springs     suddenly out of the darkness,
joyfully announcing his  presence. I am shocked and startled.
I beg him not to further complicate my life and to have pity
on me.   "Pity you ask while I adore you?  Do not speak to
me of pity!  I shall always guard your honor and respect your
blameless name," Ricardo sings.  Amelia still protests, "No
Ricardo, you must not love me nor betray your friend's
devotion.  I am the wife of the man who would gladly give
his life for yours."

[By this time in the performance, the white veil covering my
head began to slip further and further forward.  I conjectured
the bobby pins keeping it in place must have become
dislodged.  The veil was down so low in the front that I had
to hold it away from my body so I could see where I was
stepping on the darkened stage.  While singing the musical
acrobatics of the score and acting as convincingly as I could,
I struggled to reach up and reposition the pins holding the
veil. Because of its white color, I was just able to make out
Julius Rudel, the conductor, on his well-lit podium, but had to
strain to see anything else.]

A lyrical duet ensues in which Ricardo waxes romantic.  He
puts pressure on me,  "Say you love me."  I finally give up
resisting and sing very slowly,   "Ebben, si,  t'amo!," or "Well,
--- yes, I love you."  We then join together  singing in close

harmony, a lilting love duet. Ricardo continues, "With love upon us shining, we'd never seek the light of day." Having my reservations, I express the heavy weight of shame I feel and sing, "Let me end a life of shame this very day. Oh help me Lord, that I may die."

On cue, the stage lights increase in intensity as though the moon has just emerged from behind the night's passing clouds. Renato suddenly steps out of the shadows. Loyal as always, he has followed the King in order to warn him of an impending assassination attempt. Renato does not recognize me, his own veiled wife Amelia, standing near the King. I repeatedly urge Ricardo to save his own life by leaving immediately. He refuses! I threaten to create a scene by ripping off my veil if he does not go. In reaction, Ricardo then quickly asks Renato to conduct me, still veiled, safely back to town and leaves after Renato promises to protect me from all dangers. As soon as Ricardo leaves, a group of assassins arrive in search of him. They are angered not to find Ricardo but are intrigued to find Renato guarding a beautiful unknown woman whom they believe to be Ricardo's secret lady love.

[During this whole scene, I tried my best to keep my veil from falling off so that I could maintain my incognito status. I was becoming aware of the fact that gravity can play havoc with inanimate objects.]

The intruders become obsessed by finding out who I am and threaten to unveil me. Renato, sworn to protect me, pulls out his knife and sings menacingly, "Don't come near her! If you do, there will be bloodshed! --- I'll cut your throats to make you pay for any offense." Mirroring the mounting tension of this dramatic encounter, the music speeds up rhythmically into an allegro overdrive. It is a known fact that what we see, hear and sense can quicken our pulse, brain waves and rate of respiration. No one is totally immune particularly at this point in the opera!

Betty Jones

[In the story Amelia is supposed to be beside herself with fear of escalating violence and chooses to avoid it by dropping her veil. I did not! Instead, counter to the script, I fought to keep it on, thereby missing my cue to remove it. I thus inadvertently rendered the rest of this scene dramatically implausible. The words being sung did not fit my action.]

True to the musical score and drama, Renato exclaims, "What! -- Amelia!" The conspirators tease Renato by singing in a harmonic chorus, "Look how at midnight, hidden from glances, the loving paramour slyly romances! But coming near him you must not jeer him for the lively lady is his own wife. Ha Ha, Ha Ha, Ha Ha, Ha Ha. Oh how delightful a situation, oh what gossip around the town."

[How could the words have made sense to the audience when I was still an unidentified veiled lady, failing to provide the denouncement called for by the plot. Richard Fredricks, a very experienced performer, who sang the role of Renato immediately grasped the gravity of the situation. He purposefully drew nearer to me and, in a stage whisper, relayed the conductor's frantic, silent hand and lip mime. "Julius says TAKE THE VEIL OFF!" Following the line of Fredericks's riveted gaze, I was awakened to reality when I, too, deciphered the conductor's furiously gesticulative communications. Faster than greased lightening I snatched the veil from my head and balled it up out of sight in my palm, Phew! For a short while I sadly felt ridiculous, but the demands of performing in the present moment on stage quickly made short shrift of that emotion.]

As the scene progresses, the conspirators continue to ridicule Renato for having a secret liaison with his own wife, which turns his anger into rage. He turns and sings to me, "I have sworn to the King to escort you safely to the gate of town. Andiam! (let us go) Andiam!"

In the next scene the curtains open showing the study in Renato's house. He and I enter. With accelerating agitation, Renato loudly proclaims, "For this outrage, there is no pardon, Amelia, no pleading, no contrition. With your blood you will atone. You must die! Only your blood will end my shame." Overwhelmed, I fall to my knees and slowly sing a sad pleading aria, "Grant me but one mercy, that for one last time my only son can embrace me." At the end of the aria, I sing one of the most poignant melodic laments in almost all of opera, a downward arpeggio spanning my entire vocal range from high "C" to middle "C," which is two octaves. I sing with a surprisingly new freedom. Renato relents and concedes to my most desperately hoped for wish. He sings, "Kneel no more! I shall grant that to you. Go in and see your son." He also decides to pardon me for the transgressions he assumes I have committed with Ricardo but, in reality, have not.

[During the next orchestral interlude the singer Richard Fredricks used the time to again whisper in my ear, "If you ever sing like that in my presence again with such a plaintive stirring wail, I really will murder you!" and then he winked at me with the eye facing away from the audience. I thought to myself, "I've never been paid a better compliment by a colleague, but how did I ever manage to sing that difficult passage so easily and in such a soul wrenching manner? I know --- during my lament, I unwittingly slipped back into the character of Serena from Gershwin's _Porgy and Bess._ That solved it! When in doubt build on past successes either knowingly or instinctively."]

Renato decides then and there that Ricardo is the real seducer and vows to murder him instead of me. He joins forces with the assassins and, at a masked ball given by the King, Renato stabs Ricardo to death in front of all the guests. Before the King breathes his last, he uses his royal position of power to pardon all the culprits and also verbally attests to my ever present, unstained fidelity. As Ricardo staggers and teeters between life and death, one of his subjects slips a chair under him as he begins to fall. I immediately kneel close by him. The convulsive throws of approaching death overtake Ricardo, as he lurches forward in the chair, then goes limp. Renato and the other assassins sadly recant their onerous deed and everyone on stage sings, "Gracious Lord, do not deprive us of this great king." The pardoned assassins then sing in a trio, "He's dying! --- he's dying!" With his last breath and great effort, Ricardo sings, "Farewell my children forever. Farewell beloved homeland --- Oh my lord I'm dying --- my children --- farewell now."

[The dying king's agony filled death caused his chair to lurch forward and pin my dress to the floor. I had to forcefully yank my dress out from under its leg to be able to spring up to a standing position, pull out all the stops and sing the last big, very fast all cast chorus, ending the opera with, "Oh what a monstrous night! --- a night of horror!"]

After my debut performance with the New York City Opera as Amelia in <u>Un Ballo in Maschera,</u> I went on to sing many additional performances of <u>Ballo</u> over the next several years and had absolutely no problem with the persnickety veil. I just made very sure that subsequent dressers took greater care securing the veil to my hair by positioning the pins so that it would not slowly slip forward at an inopportune moment during a performance.

**Amelia - "Un Ballo In Maschera"**
**New York City Opera - (1974)**

# Mexico City Opera

After only two performances of *Un Ballo in Maschera* during my first season with the New York City Opera, I was surprised to be selected by the Chautauqua Opera Association to sing, during the summer of 1975, the very same opera again, but this time at the prestigious Music Festival located in upstate New York. Tenor, Nicholas diVirgilio and baritone Russell Christopher, both from the Metropolitan Opera, had been engaged to sing the roles of King Ricardo and his friend Renato, respectively. On learning this, I looked forward with building excitement to the prospect of making beautiful music with a real Italian tenor (diVirgilio). The performances, however, were to be sung in English instead of Italian, which meant time consuming rememorization of the entire role of Amelia. Through experience, I knew no two performances of an opera are exactly alike. Each presents different problems to be solved, while each also brings mind blowing musical gifts to enjoy and remember for the rest of one's life. I liken performing in opera to getting paid handsomely for eating a delicious ice cream sundae of one's favorite flavors.

My summer spent singing at Chautauqua strengthened my resolve to continue building a career in this profession. That fall our son Jeff returned as a student to my alma mater, Sarah Lawrence College, and daughter Janet started her freshman year at Middlebury College in Vermont. For the first time in many years, Doug and I had the entire house to ourselves. Soon I started rehearsals for my second season at the New York City Opera, where I was to sing the Countess in *The Marriage of Figaro,* more *Ballo* performances and my first major role in the German repertoire, Eva in Wagner's *Die Meistersinger.*

On a beautiful Saturday morning in early October, Doug and I picked up my parents and drove to Vermont to see Janet and attend our first Middlebury College parents weekend. As we neared her dormitory, I was surprised to see Janet streaking towards us at full gallop. Doug slammed on the brakes as Janet hastily motioned for us to roll down the windows. "Mom, Mom" she yelled, "your manager has been calling here all day. You must have told him where you were going. He said to call him back as soon as you arrive. They want you to sing in Mexico!" I immediately called my manager to get the particulars. Hans Hofmann told me, "Christina Deutekom, who was supposed to sing Amelia in _Un Ballo in Maschera_ on opening night, cancelled her performance due to sudden illness. You have been recommended to take her place at a fee of $4,500, plus airfare and hotel, for one performance. Is it possible for you to fly to Mexico City tomorrow morning?" I answered, without a moment's hesitation, "Oh yes." He then continued with a hint of relief in his voice, "Good, I'll notify Bellas Artes that you will do it and I'll make the necessary travel arrangements. Please call me as soon as you get back to Wilton. By the way, the performance will be in Italian."

Even though we were disappointed that we could not spend parents weekend with Janet, we piled back into the car and sped home to Connecticut. Since I had just sung Amelia in English at Chautauqua, I closed my eyes for most of the six hour return trip to Wilton and concentrated on going over the role in its original Italian. I could barely wait to check the accuracy of my memory against the score when at last we arrived home. To be traveling to Mexico and working on perfecting a future _Ballo_ performance was very exciting. If it had been possible to have wings, I would have flapped them and flown to Mexico ahead of the plane. On Sunday morning, Doug drove me to New York's JFK Airport. He planned to make the necessary arrangements to visit his office in Mexico City so that he could hear me sing. As I kissed him goodbye, he reminded me, "As soon as you arrive, call my local office and ask them to forward the name and telephone number of your hotel so I can keep in touch and let you know what day I'll arrive." I promised, then ran to the boarding gate.

On the flight to Mexico City, I concentrated on again studying the score in Italian. Since I had managed to survive the first and second trial by fire when I sang *Ballo* at my City Opera debut and at Chautauqua, I definitely felt more confident and less fearful attempting it a third time. After arriving at Mexico City's International Airport and going through customs, two people from La Compania Nacional de Opera de Bellas Artes greeted me, smiling, with a bouquet of flowers. As we drove to the hotel, I learned that it was one of my City Opera colleagues, Pablo Elvira, who recommended that I be retained as the replacement for Christina Deutekom. They also told me about the orchestra rehearsal scheduled for the next day. Although the conductor and I did not share any language in which we could communicate comfortably, I realized that music itself is a timeless universal language that can be enjoyed and understood by all. The conductor guides the musicians using composer's notations on the written page. Our only orchestra rehearsal went very well but, sadly, there was no time before the performance for me to learn all the staging and I prepared myself to "wing it."

Mexico City is situated at a high altitude. I wondered why I was having such trouble breathing through my nose. I thought, "What a bad time to catch a cold!" When outside the hotel, I looked around and found that there was a ground hugging hazy smog. At this high elevation, incomplete car combustion must be responsible for this foggy pollution. Easily solved! "Stay inside and keep the windows tightly closed," I told myself. My bothersome symptoms seemed to disappear as if overnight.

On my one day off, I used the handy hotel telephone book to help me get in touch with members of my father's family who had emigrated to Mexico many years ago. Contact having been made, Cousin Edmee´ asked me to have lunch with her and another family member that day. I was delighted by the prospect but made it very clear that I must, for health reasons, keep my time out of doors to a minimum. After a moment's silence, my cousin said, "There's a very good restaurant with delicious Mexican food right inside your hotel. We'll go there. I'll make reservations." "Great," I chimed back.

The waiter led us to our hastily reserved table and after we were seated, he politely handed us menus to consult. Although we had just met, my gut feeling was that I had already known these relatives for many years. Yes, we shared common genes but also certain modes of expression, speech patterns, rhythms and gestures. I felt happy and at home to be with them. The waiter returned and Edmee´ ordered for all of us. A short while later, the waiter reappeared, balancing our steaming aromatic plates of delicacies. After a toast with Tequila, Edmee´ and my other relative lustily dug into their food as soon as it was placed in front of them. What were we eating anyway? At closer inspection of my plate, I saw crescents of meat nestled in a creamy brown gravy. I ventured a little taste. "Yum," I hummed and said, while politely wiping my lips with a napkin, "Thank you Edmee´ for ordering for me. Since the menu is all in Spanish, I wouldn't have had a clue as to what to ask for. It's really quite delicious! Oh by the way, what's it called?" Edmee´ replied, "It's a Mexican specialty, listed on the menu as 'Criadillas,' but in other parts of the Spanish speaking world it is called by different names. 'Huevos de Toro' is one of those most frequently used." "I see," I continued, "but what is it really made of?" After a long pregnant silence and a deep intake of air, Edmee´ answered slowly, "It's made of a bull's testicles in gravy." "What?" I thought silently to myself, so that I would not insult them, "You've got to be kidding, Ha!" Then I said aloud, "Very interesting" and quickly changed the subject. "Oh well, at the Village Market in my home town of Wilton you can also buy exotic foods like canned chocolate-covered ants. I hear they are crunchy wonderful."

After lunch, I returned to my hotel room to rest up and wait for Doug, who was flying in that afternoon to attend my performance the next day. I also silently sang through the entire opera before falling asleep. At long last, Doug finally arrived accompanied by Ed Farias, the manager of his company's local office. I had met Ed previously. He and his secretary were helpful when I first arrived in Mexico. He wanted to take us to dinner at his club but, since I had a performance the next evening and needed my rest, we had an early dinner at the same hotel restaurant I had earlier been to with my relatives. During dinner, Ed said, "Make sure you are paid in U.S. dollars rather than pesos because of the lower exchange rate." He added, "My wife and I are looking forward to being present and cheering you on when you sing tomorrow night."

**Opening Night - La Compania Nacional de Opera de Bellas Artes**
**"Ballo in Maschera"**
**Mexico City (1975)**

The next evening's performance went swimmingly well. At intermission between the third and fourth acts, they tried to pay me in my dressing room the fee of $4,500 in bills of small denominations. I was asked to sign I had received the money. "Where can I hide this big pile of precious green stuff, all in $5 and $10 dollar bills, while I'm on stage?" I did not feel it would be safe to leave it in my dressing room unguarded, so I prevailed upon the stage manager to call Doug out of the audience. A voice on the loud speaker asked Doug in English to come backstage immediately. His first thought was that something terrible had happened to me. "Oh my God, maybe she's dropped dead or something?" When he arrived backstage, he was relieved to find that I was all right. After Doug counted the money for me, I signed the receipt. He then stuffed his pockets with the cash and returned to his seat a much fatter guy and heaving an all's well sigh of relief.

Finally the end of the opera arrived and it was time for us all to take our bows. The chorus, comprimarios and other singers hurried to their pre-planned designated spots on stage to await the audience's recognition. From the other side of the curtain all the artists could hear loud clapping and cheering. Waiting in the dark wings on either side of the stage were those who sang principal roles, lined up in order of ascending importance. Since Amelia is a major role, I was one of the last to take my bows. I stood there out of sight, watching the lights begin to flood a stage full of performers as the curtains slowly parted.

Most physical movements in opera around the world are based on suitably stylized classical dance. Not so in Mexico! Here they harken to a different drumbeat when they take their bows. As I watched them from the wings, my mouth slowly fell open in awe and incredulity. Their templates were the movements of a matador in the bull fight ring. When it was their turn to soak up the audiences adulation, they strutted on stage one by one and assumed easily recognizable stances.   The only thing missing was the red cape used to incite the bull to attack.   With mounting excitement, the audience responded in kind.   When it was my turn to take my bows, I knew that I could not even approach the Spanish singer's stylization. I just accepted the audiences honor the only way I knew, simply and gracefully. To hear the audience clap even louder for me touched my heart with joy.

# Singing in Europe

Preparing for an operatic career became my number one priority. I felt that I needed, among other things, to familiarize myself with the three languages in which opera is usually written, namely French, German, and Italian. I asked friends in Wilton and Westport if they knew of anyone who would work with me in this regard. On my own, I started studying German at night in a continuing education program at our local Wilton High School. Luckily, a French teacher materialized and we moved forward in that language on a one-on-one basis.

Through one of my contacts, I heard about a travel agent named Sandra Capsis, who in her off hours taught Italian. At our first scheduled meeting, she greeted me with a warm hello and hug. I conjectured that she must have been born and raised in Italy, where opera singers are held in high regard. We liked each other from the moment we met and became good friends. I asked her to please translate into English word for word, roles that I was studying. As we worked, she also became more and more interested in helping me succeed in my singing career. At the conclusion of one lesson, Sandra confided in me, "Betty dear, I have a friend in New York named Sarah Keene who I'd like to have you sing for. Her husband is a brilliant, up and coming young conductor. If she likes what she hears, I'm sure she'll speak to him about you. Here's her telephone number." The most baffling part of this turn of events is that Sandra had never heard me sing! She must have based her decision to mentor me on an intuitive reaction alone. In this instance "...Luck was the lady..." she is touted to be. Sarah Keene liked my voice and asked me to return to sing for her husband, Christopher.

After I sang for Christopher Keene, he concurred with his wife and immediately made arrangements for an audition with noted composer Gian Carlo Menotti. The first opera role I ever sang was Madame Flora in Menotti's *The Medium* at the Wilton Playshop. I did not know that Menotti had embarked on a talent search to find and engage soloists to sing the Benjamin Britten *War Requiem* in a large scale outdoor concert which was to be the closing event of the 1973 Spoleto Festival in Italy. Christopher Keene had already been engaged by Menotti to conduct. I sang for Menotti along with other hopefuls at a New York rehearsal studio. Fortunately, I received his approval and my manager was subsequently sent a contract.

Spoleto Festival
Italy (1973)

The fates looked favorably on me when Doug was able to arrange his schedule and accompany me on my first European engagement. Let us fast forward now on the film of life to our arrival, bags in hand, in Spoleto, Italy. We were taken to our lodgings. The prospective audience of "Festival dei Due Mondi" (Festival of the Two Worlds) had already filled every hotel in town to the brim. We were rescued by nuns in a convent. The room they rented to us was quite small and the building was on a treacherously precipitous hill with a surprise right angle curve at the bottom. Our first night there we were awakened many times by the flash of car lights through the windows, illuminating our room,

140

and the loud screech of tires as brakes were hastily applied at the bottom of the road's radically oblique turn. Each time we heard the screech, we anticipated the ominous sound of a car crash, but we never heard one and so slipped back to sleep. If at any time we ventured to entertain amorous inclinations, they were quickly chilled by the thought of thin convent walls and the discovery that the bed constantly complained by squeaking loudly. Our self imposed celibacy finally came to an end after three days when the small apartment originally reserved for us at last became vacant. We both heaved a happy sigh of relief. Our new quarters were right next to those of conductor Christopher Keene and his wife Sarah.

To do justice to the many aspects of the _War Requiem_ is a leviathan endeavor. There are three soloists: soprano, tenor and baritone, accompanied by a full symphony orchestra and a smaller chamber group, a boys choir and a large adult chorus, all of whom had to be rehearsed separately and in sequence. With all the work that had to be accomplished, two weeks went by quickly. Using the "Mass for the Dead" in Latin as the main theme, Britten interspersed settings of poems written in English and German by Wilfred Owen that recount, with refined fiery elegance, wars senseless butchery.

> "My subject is war, and the pity of war
> the poetry is in the pity.........
> all a poet can do today is warn"

The most poignant part of the work occurs when two soldiers from opposing sides meet after death. One says to the other in song, "I am the enemy you killed, my friend." This epic masterpiece begins with "Requiem aeternam dona eis Domine" (Eternal rest grant unto them God). At the very end the two soldiers a tenor and a baritone quietly sing together, "Let us sleep now."

We welcomed the sunny, mild day of the performance with gleeful anticipatory excitement. This was to be the last in the series of festival concerts taking place outdoors in the Piazza del Duomo, the Cathedral Square. Menotti owned an apartment which overlooked the square and it was his charming custom, with gallant flourish to escort the performing soloists, down the center aisle bisecting the audience, to their place upon the stage just before the concert begins. As I took my assigned seat in front of the orchestra, I was awed by the huge number of the audience. There were approximately 8,000 people present, and every eye was glued on me and the other soloists. This was certainly the largest audience that I had yet been blessed to sing for. I was determined not to shrink in fear from the magnitude of this task but to enjoy it in style. So, I put on my best smile and looked around in order to record everything I could for future reference. The orchestra tuned up and the concert got underway. While waiting for my first music cue, my attention was drawn to the blue sky overhead and the white cotton candy clouds slowly drifting by at high altitude. Just below them flew a large flock of birds in formation, as if paying just homage to the Requiem's war dead. I reasoned that possibly they were drawn by the sound of the music, because they circled and twittered throughout the entire concert.

All of my solos were in the liturgical Latin of the Catholic Mass for the dead, accompanied by either the adult chorus or the boys choir. Latin is a good language to sing in because it is the basis of all the romance languages, the vowels are pure and it brings out the very best sounding voice possible.

When the huge audience responded to the beauty of the music by loudly clapping their approval, it was like thunder without the attendant rain, wind and darkness. High on a round green hill, off to the left, was a long one story concrete building. As my eyes adjusted, I became aware of the fact that there were visible hands clasping bars at each window. I thought to myself in disbelief, it must be a prison. How fortunate the confined were close enough to hear, see and enjoy this open air concert as non-paying audience members.

I will bet that Sing Sing Penitentiary prisoners in the United States have never been lucky enough to be treated to such a lovely spiritual gift.

The War Requiem ends very quietly after 179 pages of heart rending poetry and music. It is an intersession plea asking that all those who have died in battle rest in peace. Many bows were taken as a long, loud applause arose from the audience continued and then abated into near silence. No one seemed to make a move to leave. They just stood there and quietly waited. Waited for what? One of the soloists leaned in my direction and whispered, "They are waiting for Gian-Carlo Menotti to escort the conductor and soloists back through the audience to his apartment." After this was done, our appearance together framed by the window elicited renewed excited cheers, applause and energetic arm waving from the audience. We acknowledged their appreciative warmth and recognition by responding in kind. Menotti complimented me on my voice and my interpretation of the music. In parting he said thoughtfully, "I'd like to write something special for you to sing." I thanked him assiduously for this honor.

After we exchanged greetings with the audience from Menotti's apartment window, he invited us all to his nearby castle to celebrate his birthday. Delicious food and wine were served. Champagne flowed like water, but water was a rarer commodity. It was the dry season and one could only get water from the tap during certain hours of the day. Being able to flush the toilets after use waxed and wained because of the over use by so many guests in town.

At the party in Menotti's castle, one particularly beautiful girl, exuding charm, found a comfortable seat next to Doug. He asked her out of curiosity, "What do you do around here." She pondered the question for a moment, due to her limited familiarity with English, then answered hesitantly with a strong Italian accent, "I do anything Gian Carlo asks me to do."

The day after the concert, reviewer George Mott from the Daily American wrote this headline:   "OPEN PIAZZA PROVES UNSUITABLE SETTING FOR BRITTEN'S WAR REQUIEM".  He continued,

> ".....Last night the Piazza del Duomo of Spoleto with its noisy over-excited audience, wheeling screeching birds and variable acoustics offered insurmountable difficulties to an already difficult task of realizing the composer's vision of war as savage inhumanity expressed with chilling restraint....."

Mott found fault with almost everything until he reached my singing.  He then wrote:

> ".....The soprano Betty Jones was a joy to hear in this music. The 'Lacrimosa' was memorable.  Her warm powerful voice glimmering with silver at the top soared effortlessly over the chorus and orchestra....."

## TOSCA:
Giacomo Puccini's _Tosca_ was originally written in Italian.  I had studied this major role with my voice teacher in that language.  She also insisted that I  study many of the other great soprano roles in my vocal category, just in case --- but who could forsee having to sing _Tosca,_ on short notice in an entirely different foreign language?  My managers called one day and told me that they had heard of a chance to sing _Tosca_ in Wiesbaden Germany.  They then asked, "Can you fly over and audition as soon as possible?   We can set up other auditions for you in nearby places as well."  A "Yes" joyfully bubbled up in my throat.

I flew to Germany for the audition and was promptly engaged by the Wiesbaden Hessischer Staats Opera to sing my first _Tosca_.  They handed me a copy of the score that they were using. I was stunned to find that the opera was to be sung in a new German translation and not in Italian. Soon after my arrival I began to experience a thrilling new career phenomenon --- for the first time, singing engagements in the United States began to pile up. After a contract for _Tosca_ was signed, I flew back home from Germany because one of my first engagements was to sing a benefit concert in Chicago for my alma mater, Sarah Lawrence College. On the return flight to Connecticut my bag, with my precious score in German, was evidently lost. After much searching through mountains of lost baggage in an airport warehouse, I learned my lesson well and NEVER AGAIN packed my music in checked luggage. My managers made an SOS call overseas and I breathed a sigh of relief when a few days later, a replacement score arrived. Because my time to memorize _Tosca_ in German was very short, the score never left my hands except when I slept. My performance responsibilities in the U.S. having been met, I was then free to travel and return to Germany to begin rehearsals in earnest. Thank goodness for the airlines. They almost made it possible to be in two places at once.

Over a three year period, the Wiesbaden Hessischen Staatstheater had just been newly refurbished at a cost of over $80 million. The theater's ceiling was a painted fairyland of colorful scenes lit by glittering crystal chandeliers and inhabited by carved flying cherubs. The newly expanded backstage area was as big as an airplane hanger and contained the most up-to-date stage devices. There was also a large special employee lounge with comfortable chairs and an intimate bar so that the cast could relax and socialize together during rehearsal breaks. A line of bubbling amber colored glasses of beer was always drawn ahead of time and awaited the next enslaught of singers, dancers and stagehands. I felt secure and pleased by the way I was being so thoroughly rehearsed, both musically and dramatically. At last, I really felt quite ready to perform the demanding role of Tosca.

While in Wiesbaden, I lived in a small hotel called the

Einhorn, which was near the opera house, and ate in restaurants alone with my always open opera score. The traditional German cuisine was served along with bread and instead of butter, a spread of rendered grey fat. For variety, I searched the area until I found an Italian restaurant. I escaped and ate there when I felt the need for the taste of Latin food and a warm relaxed atmosphere. The maitre d' greeted me on my first arrival at the door with a smile, exclaiming, "Oh bella donna (beautiful lady), we're so happy to welcome and serve you." I was doubly pleased to discover that they served only butter with their bread!

The story of the opera *Tosca* was based on a play written by Victorien Sardou and is set in the 1800's, when Italy was besieged by Napoleon. Tosca is in love with the painter Mario Cavaradossi, who by day works up on a scaffold painting a portrait of the "Magdalena" in the Church of Saint Andrea della Valle. During rehearsal I could not understand why, when I arrived Mario was staged to come down only a few steps from the scaffold to greet me. This handsome singer was quite tall and had to practically bend over double in order to embrace me. It was not until very near the first performance that I learned the reason why. The Mario with whom I had been rehearsing was only the cover and would not be singing the actual performances. When the lead tenor arrived to take over, I noted that I was taller than he, so it was essential that this Mario stand a few steps higher on the stairs in order that we now could be closer to the same height and more believable as lovers.

The role of Tosca seemed to have been written especially for me. Tosca and I both flamboyantly express our thoughts and reactions from our very core, because we are both opera singers. She is also loving, strong emotionally, and full of spit, fire, and vinegar.

Angelotti, an escaped prisoner has just come to Mario in the church for temporary safe asylum. The Chief of Police,

146

Scarpia, is in hot pursuit. Scarpia arrests and tortures Mario to find out where he has spirited Angelotti into hiding. I, too, have been summoned to Scarpia's headquarters. On my arrival, I find him relaxing at his elegant, long dinner table with a glass of red wine in hand. He offers me some wine. I refuse to drink it as I sit ramrod straight on the other side of the table, dressed in a long dark green velvet dress. As he sips, he questions me. I am shaken when suddenly I hear Mario's scream in pain from a nearby torture chamber. To make matters worse, I am told by Scarpia that my beloved will soon be executed and that only I can save him by divulging Angelotti's hiding place and promising Scarpia that I will let him make love to me. This last request is more than my character can bear. I stand up but my knees begin to weaken. I stumble forward and fall face down on the stage floor. It is time now for me to sing one of the most famous and beautiful arias in all of opera, "Vissi d'arte." How do I see the conductor when I am lying in such a position? In Weisbaden, a camera trained on the conductor sends images to 2-TV monitors hidden on stage behind the curtains. All I have to do when falling is to make sure that I can see one of them when I land. In addition, the maestro in the pit also carefully watches Tosca's breathing until he sees her inhale fully, as a singer does in preparation to sing. Then he cues the orchestra to begin this prayerfull aria. In "Vissi d'arte," I enumerate the many loving and compassionate devotions I have poured out to the greater glory of the Lord. I ask, "Why, oh why God, do you remunerate me in this way?" Scarpia walks around to my side of the table as I slowly rise. I quickly reach for a sharp knife that is part of the dinnerware on the table and hide it behind me. I give lip service to his demands, but, when Scarpia closes in to press his advantage, singing, "Tosca, you are finally mine!" I stab him to death, shouting, "This --- is the kiss of Tosca!"

**"Tosca" Wiesbaden, Germany (1978)**

**"Tosca" Wiesbaden, Germany (1978)**

Every major character also dies before the end of this opera. My Mario is executed by a firing squad, although Scarpia has handed me a safe conduct letter to help us escape after what he said would be Mario's faux execution. But the bullets are real and in retribution Scarpia then dies by my hand. The escaped hidden prisoner, Angelotti, commits suicide and I sing my last line before I join Mario in death by throwing myself off a parapet, crying out threateningly, "Oh Scarpia --- we'll meet before God!"

After the performance I took my bows with the rest of the cast. Then, as is the custom, I received the waiting admirers one by one in the green room. Among them was a familiar face. "It's Aunt Gladys," I squealed, my father's sister who lived in the nearby town of Mainz. With joyful recognition I motioned to her to "Come! Give me a hug." How wonderful to see someone I know. Behind her, proud and smiling, was Doug. When at last all the hoopla was over and we were quietly alone, Doug confided in me, "You were wonderful tonight, Sweetie Pie! Boy --- you sang a lot of German and such beautiful high notes. I was so excited about you that when I went to the men's room to relieve myself during intermission, I was very thankful that I was the only person in my cubicle."

Reviews of my performance appeared in two local newspapers on September 18, 1978. The Wiesbadener Stadnachrichten wrote (translated from German):

> ".....Betty Jones's performance in the title role clearly became richer as the evening progressed. With her highly emotional acting intensity, she was able to elicit during the second act, the only sustained applause and rightly so, from a very reserved audience....."

In the Wiesbadener Kurier, the reviewer, wrote:

".....This time around, the American singer, Betty Jones played this intense but attractive role. With her more sensitive, adaptable and soft modulating voice rather than an exuberantly gushing soprano, she was able to impart a human dimension to the role. She conformed less to the emotional ebullience of the opera than to the lyrical expectations, whereby her prayer "Vissi d'arte" was embedded as a memory filled song in the horror filled Scarpia Act. One was able to experience Betty Jones's Tosca as a love romance that was intimate, sentimental, and touched by a degree of happiness but at the same time also overshadowed by tragedy....."

# New York City Opera (Continued)

### THE MARRIAGE OF FIGARO:

After singing two performances of _Un Ballo in Maschera_ and covering three others during my first season with the New York City Opera, I went on to spend the next seven years happily performing major roles with this wonderful company. During my second season, I was assigned the role of the Countess in Mozart's _The Marriage of Figaro_, not as an understudy or a member of the second cast but as a member in the much coveted first cast that included Samuel Ramey as Figaro and Kathleen Battle as Susanna.

As soon as I heard which role I had been engaged to sing, I hurried to the music store to buy the score, so that I could begin to work it into my voice and also commit it to memory as soon as possible. In aviation, for every hour a plane flies in the air mechanics have worked on it many hours on the ground beforehand. It is the same with learning a role. Singers need a lot of quiet downtime in order to flawlessly prepare themselves. Now you have the answer to an age old riddle --- why do opera singers get so fat? During our long hours of intense study --- WE EAT! In the past, obesity was thought to be one of the main requirements in the production of a fabulously rich well-rounded sound. Today, if one presents one's self for consideration with an overly ample physique, one probably will not get engaged or worse --- will possibly even get fired. I never had a weight problem but I was quite tall (5'-11") and towered over the usually shorter tenors. The lighter the opera, the smaller are the voices needed to sing it and the shorter the stature of the performers. Conversely, Verdi and Wagner composed dynamically much heavier music, than Mozart, so the tenor who is the usual love interest of the reigning soprano in these operas would usually be either my height or taller.

In 1785, Mozart, then at the height of his powers as a composer, felt a burning desire to show the world what he could do in an Italian opera. He and the librettist Lorenzo da Ponte discussed the possible adaptation of a Beaumarchais stage play, _The Marriage of Figaro,_ to an opera. Mozart was intrigued by Beaumarchais's treatment of the clever, comical convolutions and involutions of the complicated plot. Every character hides behind a socially acceptable facade, a secret agenda of one type or another. In the story, the Countess suspects that her husband, the Count has a roving eye. She is pretty sure he is interested in Susanna, her chambermaid, who is betrothed to Figaro, the Count's valet. The plot revolves around the Countess trying to embarrass the Count into behaving himself, so that the Count and Countess can regain their former marital fidelity and Figaro and Susanna will marry and live happily ever after.

There were serious obstacles in the way of Mozart's accomplishing his dream. Before the opera was written, the Viennese Emperor forbade any company to perform it in public, even as a play, much less an opera. He said it was "much too outspoken for polite audiences." In France, Beaumarchais faced similar problems. Performances were permitted only in private homes, not in public theaters. By word of mouth, however, the play quickly became a resounding success despite the restrictions placed on it. Beaumarchais's play shamelessly pokes fun at the dissoluteness of the upper classes, which is why there was such trepidation concerning performing it under the cloak of a "gay and witty comedic intrigue." Power was placed in the hands of elite, undeserving men merely because they were born into upper class society.

Mozart and the librettist da Ponte began collaborating on the opera in October 1785 and finished writing it six months later. By April 29, 1786, _The Marriage of Figaro_ was ready to be performed in its naughty entirety. Owing to its unexpected grass roots success, those critical of the plot gradually withdrew their complaints, and It has become a favorite of opera lovers ever since, all over the world.

This was to be my first of many portrayals of the sophisticated, wise and beautiful Countess that I would sing during my career. I did not know, however, that I would have to do my first performance without the benefit of either a stage or orchestra rehearsal, both of which for reasons unknown to me had to be cancelled at the last minute. To add to the mayhem, I had never worn the costume before. The stage director felt obligated to quickly apprise City Opera Director Julius Rudel of the situation. Rudel calmed his own fears by answering, "I know what Betty Jones can do --- she'll be just fine!"

Coutness - "Marriage of Figaro"
New York City Opera (1976)

That night, just before curtain time, the stage director escorted me on stage for the first time so that he could familiarize me with the set. He said, "Here on the table are the Countess's comb and brush." I thought to myself, "Pick them up, --- hold them, Betty, and press them close to you. Feel them well with your hands! They've been used by you for many a year." Pointing as he continued to explain, "Over here are three curtained French doors. You stand alone next to them when you sing your first aria in Act ll." I agreed, "Yes, the one where I lament my husband the Count's unfaithfulness." As I stood there, I ran over the words of the prayer in my mind and visualized myself on stage singing the aria "Porgi Amor" in performance. Translated into English the words are, "Pour, O Love, sweet consolation on my lonely broken heart. Oh give me back his lost affection or I beg you, let me die! Bring me comfort in my suffering, hear my broken hearted sigh. Give me back my Lord and husband or I beg you to let me die."

The stage director continued our last minute tour. "Here is the door you exit through. It only opens outwards so don't try to pull it towards you because it won't budge. The bush beyond the door is filled with beautiful flowers. You are supposed to pick one as you pass by but only this one here (he pointed to it) will come off in your hand. The others are permanently attached."

There was one situation that I had to solve without outside coaching help. The long dining table on which my comb and brush were placed held two unlit candelabras and, dining chairs were drawn up close to it. The director told me to walk along its full length in the space between the table and the chairs. Before the opening performance, one of the stage crew lit the candles as he was directed to do. I was struck numb with horror when I came on stage just before the performance to find that the chairs were placed so close to the table that I could envision the candle flames frying my nippled orbs as I tried to slip by unscathed. As it turned out, my fears were groundless. All went well and no one had to use the fire extinguisher on me and interrupt the performance. The wise stage hands had left just enough room for me to squeeze by.

An hour later, the curtain rose all too soon on the performance. My character does not come on stage until the beginning of the second act when I sing the reminiscent aria of longing for my husband's pure love of the past. The orchestra prepares the audience for what is to follow by musically previewing the slow, sweet melodic themes before I sing them. Mozart really knew how to compose for the solo instrument, in this case the voice. At no time did he ever cover my sound with the orchestration. In the accompaniment, he wrote many rest marks per measure so that the singer can quietly caress the melody as it rises and falls, yet always be heard and remain in the spotlight.

A Broadway show is usually written to include the spoken dialogue of the story between songs. Not so in opera. The words, or recitatives, are most always set to music. The intrigue of such an intricately woven opera plot like *The Marriage of Figaro* needs to be shared with the audience by the characters and thoroughly understood to be effective. Every voice category (soprano, mezzo, tenor, and bass) sing in a different register. Sopranos sing way up high with ease while mezzos sing in mid-range. Tenors sing high for a man and basses round out the bottom. Recitatives may ease the listener's ear unknowingly from one key to the different key of the next aria, and some go on for many pages at a time. They are invaluable when trying to understand what is about to happen on stage. For example, in order to catch the Count in his sculduggerys, the Countess takes Susanna into her confidence. They exchange outfits and plan, in a lengthy conversation set to music, a rendezvous with the Count. Sure enough, the Count tries to make a move on the one who he thinks is Susanna but is really his own wife, the Countess. Once exposed, he humbly begs his wife's pardon, which she grants, and so the opera ends on a happy note.

Mozart arias are to be sung in a very genteel classic form. There are none of the Italian opera's hot blooded pyrotechnics. Some months before the City Opera performance, I had the opportunity to audition in Germany, singing an aria from *Figaro.* A critique was shared with me afterwards. I was told that I had sung the aria in an altogether too Italianate style, causing the opera company not to engage me. Once warned, I was conscious from then on of the different composer's styles and even the year in which the opera was written. There is no substitute for experience.

Because I had had no stage or orchestra rehearsal before my first Figaro, I was under a lot of stress. As I was rushing to my dressing room after Act lll, Julius Rudel, who was backstage during the performance, said to me, "Miss Jones, I do believe this role is right for you but do you realize you are sometimes singing flat." My answer was, "Do you realize Maestro this is the first time I'm hearing the orchestra" and with a muffled sob I quickly ran down the hall. When the curtain finally came down after the all cast Act IV finale, which goes on for 60 pages, I felt a lot better as I took my bows. Back at the hotel I unwound in a most unhealthy manner by staying up most of that night and crying in the bathroom. I thought my career at the City Opera was over. Doug came in to comfort me saying, "Sweetie, that was just your dress rehearsal. You're leaving in the morning to sing _Aida_ in Seattle and when you return for your next performance of _Figaro_, I'm sure you will be fine." I finally said to myself, "Oh well, you can't win them all! This one is only the beginning." I then went to bed and slept soundly the rest of the night, with hope reinplanted in my heart. Emotional resilience is a must in this artistic business.

## DIE MEISTERSINGER VON NÜRNBERG:
As a Connecticut reviewer once said, "Emergencies are the stuff of which opportunity is made." Saturday evening, September 25, 1976, on less than 24 hours notice, I had to take over from the ailing Johanna Meier the leading role of Eva in Wagner's _Die Meistersinger_ (Mastersinger). Since there was no time for either a full staging or orchestra rehearsal, the City Opera's Conductor Julius Rudel, the essence of professionalism, coached my staging and orchestra cues.

Before the performance, costumers feverishly fitted this tall soprano with 17th century costumes, blonde wig and a gala wedding gown. Beverly Sills, the well known artist who was scheduled to take over as Director of the City Opera, knocked on my dressing room door. "Come in!" I yelled. "Betty," she said quietly as she entered, "I've come to check out your costumes and shoes."

Eva - "Die Meistersinger"
New York City Opera (1976)

I was deeply touched when she immediately got down on the floor on all fours. "Um---," she ruminated. "The dress length seems to be all right," she was relieved to discover. It had been let down as far as it could go. "What about the shoes?" she asked. "We figured they'd be a little too small for you. To be on the safe side, we sprayed them with special stuff so they would stretch larger to fit your feet if needed. Remember, we're all pulling for you," she continued. "Gain courage from the fact that if you weren't able to go on, the show would have had to be cancelled. Your presence and performance is saving the evening from a total disaster." Satisfied that most everything fit, she said just before leaving, "I'll tell the costumers they need to refit the waist before you go on, though. It seems a little too tight to sing in."

Just before the curtain rose, a member of the sewing brigade came to my dressing room to tackle the last of my costume problems. Over the intercom I could hear the orchestra starting to tune up as she quickly removed the stitching from the bodice. "All right now --- take in your full breath like you do when you're singing. Get as big as you usually do," the seamstress suggested. She quickly pinned the dress back together and threaded her needle. As she was sewing me into the dress, I heard the beginning of the overture being played. "Boy, she'd better hurry up and get finished!" I thought to myself. I guess she must have read the anxious expression on my face. "Don't worry," she said intuitively, "It takes the orchestra a full half hour to play the whole overture. We still have plenty of time to fix everything that needs fixing!"

As soon as she was through sewing, I hurried to take my place on stage. Up went the curtain on cue and I was able to connect with the darkened full house audience. Electrical energy that coursed thru my blood and brain, brought on by a build up of anticipatory performance exhilaration, finally passed out of my body in song. No more flashes from this, as yet unconnected, sparking live wire. I was then able to direct my full energy to enliven the psyches and souls of the listeners sitting out front. What a relief!

The first scene takes place in Nuremberg, Germany at St. Katharine's Church. The singing congregation (chorus) numbers about 76. As the opera progresses, there are dancers and townfolk in subsequent scenes. So you can see, this is a very large cast. The score itself is 569 pages and takes approximately five hours to perform in its entirety.

Eva and Walther (a knight) have fallen in love. Eva's father has, however, pledged her hand to whoever wins the Mastersingers song contest. Walther decides to enter the competition in the hopes of winning as the prize his beloved's hand in marriage. Although he too loves Eva, Hans Sachs, a member of the Shoemaker's Guild and already a

Mastersinger himself, shepherds Walther through the contest. As Eva, I then sing my one big aria of praise, "O Sachs Mein Freund" (O Sachs my friend). My dearest one, how can I thank you for all you have done." These words took on special meaning a short time after I sang them. I never could have finished the performance without the cobbler's expert intervention. I had noticed that as the contestant Beckmesser sang, Sachs critiqued his bad performance with mocking hammer blows on a shoe he was supposedly repairing. Now the shoes that I was wearing fit well (thanks to the shoe spray) but one heel felt disconcertingly loose. At the start of the intermission, I took it off and to my horror discovered the heel was just about to fall off. I rushed over to Sachs on stage and explained my predicament. "Give it here, Betty," he said with a blithe smile. "Opera singing is my real profession but I'm hoping that with a few good wacks I'll be able to fix your shoe as well!" He banged the heel with his stage prop hammer until magically it was securely reattached. He then proudly returned the shoe to me saying incredulously, "Can you believe it? I did it! Whoopie!"

**"Die Meistersinger"**
**With John Alexander as Walther**

Near the end of the opera, Eva's true love Walther sings his beautiful tenor aria "The Prize Song" and wins the Mastersinger contest. Their dream of marrying and his membership in the Guild would now come to pass, a happy ending to the glory of German Guild art. Whenever Eva thinks of Walther or Walther thinks of Eva, the romantic melody of the Prize song repeatedly wafts through the orchestra. John Alexander, whom I first met in Boston, sang the role of Walther in this

particular production, and to this day, whenever I think of
*Die Meistersinger* and the Prize Song melody, his voice sings in
my mind and warms my heart. Because my performance was
a success, I was assigned to sing it for three additional
performances as a member of the first cast. Before this
opportunity arrived, however, the City Opera Orchestra went
on strike, sadly causing the cancellation of the remaining
season . C'est la vie! C'est la vie.

## DER FLIEGENDE HOLLÄNDER (THE FLYING DUTCHMAN):

In 1975, Wagner's *The Flying Dutchman* was performed by
Opera/South, an all Black company, at the City Auditorium
in Jackson, Mississippi. The venerable, white Walter Herbert
of the San Diego Opera was the conductor. This audacious
young company in only its fifth season had been named by
The New York Times "Who's Who in Opera" one of the
nation's top 34 opera companies.    After a lengthy audition
process, I was engaged to sing the leading role of Senta in
this production.    Frank Haines, the Arts Editor of the
Jackson Daily News, wrote of my performance on April 21,
1975:

> "....THINGS CAME GENUINELY ALIVE IN
> ACT II with the introduction of the superbly exciting
> singer with the unbefitting plebeian name of Betty
> Jones.  Names, however, become what is invested in
> them, I shouldn't wonder if "Betty Jones" will not
> one day strike us as an exceedingly  glamorous name,
> for Miss Jones is something else. Hers is the kind of
> rich , vibrant soprano which seems to have no  limit
> to the bottom or top but floats easily and clearly
> through the registers. It is one of the most gripping
> vocal presences I've encountered lately: dramatically,
> Miss Jones does not yet have a command to match
> the voice but I feel it's there to be tapped. She's a
> strikingly handsome woman, with all the potential for
> a great Wagnerian soprano......"

The experience I gained at that time would prove to be invaluable to me in the future. A year and a half later, while working on a role with my colleagues and a coach at the New York City Opera, someone from the management flung the door wide open and rushed in. He seemed to be in an very agitated state as he breathlessly blurted out, "Anyone here know the role of Senta in Wagner's _The Flying Dutchman?_" I piped up promptly, "Oh yes, I do." He then said, as he was leaving, "Please come to the office as soon as you're finished here."

When my rehearsal ended, I hurried to the office as requested. There I was told that Johanna Meir, who was scheduled to sing Senta in a few days, cancelled and that her cover, Earline Ballard, had just hurt herself badly on stage. In the last scene of this opera, Senta is supposed to jump to her death, throwing herself off a cliff into the sea. During the dress rehearsal, Miss Ballard miscalculated how far down the mattress which, was supposed to break her fall, had been placed. Thinking she had more space to fall than she actually did, she jumped with legs straight and knees locked, causing painful injuries to both her legs. She was ordered by the doctor to healing bedrest and the call went out immediately to find another artist to perform the role. Her sad misfortune became my joyful opportunity. Performing on stage can be very dangerous if something goes wrong, even to the point of becoming life threatening. You have to keep your wits about you every second of the time you are there. All efforts were made to quickly prepare me in every way to safely take on the role of Senta, which I was now scheduled to perform in just two days. All my other rehearsals were immediately cancelled and two coaches were assigned to me so I could begin the process of rememorization of the role.

In the opera, Senta is in love with the Flying Dutchman. He and his ship have been cursed by the devil to ply the oceans of the world, allowed to put into port for a short while just once every seven years. Only the pure love of a faithful woman can ever free him from this endless treadmill of torture. In the orchestration of the overture, certain themes of the famous arias are previewed, giving the audience a foretaste of what is to follow. Most of the opera takes place on the waterfront where ships dock. To add to the veracity of this allegorical plot, Wagner treats us to music which rolls and pitches like ocean waves. He sometimes conjures up raging storms and at other times the peace of ocean stillness.

As Senta, I have the opportunity to explain in my first aria my loving fixation on the beleagered Flying Dutchman. I sing in German, "Yet this pallid man from his lifelong curse may still be delivered. Find a maiden faithful and true to love him forever. I would be she, who by my love will save thee! Oh may God's angel hither guide thee. Through me may new found joy betide thee!"

**Senta - "The Flying Dutchman"**
**Opera/South, Jackson Mississippi (1975)**

162

Erik, a hunter has unwisely fallen in love with me and expects to marry me but I am determined to remain faithful to my Dutchman.   As Erik and I seriously discuss this matter further, the Dutchman overhears our conversation. He begins to feel betrayed and gives up his quest for freedom through me.  Sadly, he calls for his crew to unfurl the sails and weigh anchor.  As he and his ship begin to sail out of port, they magically disappear into the mist.   I am heartsick at the thought of losing him forever.   I dash towards a rocky cliff overlooking the sea, planning to throw myself to my death and thus proving how much I care and thereby freeing him from his curse forever.

During the performance I arrived at the place in the opera where Earline Ballard suffered her unfortunate mishap.  The closer I came to the rocky ledge, the more frightened I became about leaping off the edge of this precipice.   I strained my eyes, trying to gauge where I would land.  No wonder Earline had her troubles.  I could dimly see a single bed mattress below, but it was covered in black velvet making it virtually disappear into the dark recesses of the set.   I could, however, see clearly that there were two muscular men on either side of the mattress who motioned me to  "Come on --- jump!  You can do it!"  I took them at their word. Throwing caution to the wind, I jumped, landing in the arms of the two young stagehands, a surprisingly pleasurable experience.  I was safe and unharmed thanks to them.  Since Senta has now proved her unswerving faithfulness, the black spell cast on the Dutchman is forever broken and, as the curtain closes, the audience sees our embracing apparition float off heavenward over the sea.

This new production of _The Flying Dutchman_ by the New York City Opera was reviewed by the New York Times on October 25, 1976.   John Rockwell wrote of  my unexpected performance:

".....The Senta was Betty Jones filling in at the last moment for Earline Ballard, who was to have replaced Johanna Meir, but who tore ligaments in both ankles leaping from a balustrade in rehearsal. Miss Jones has the right vocal material for the part --- at its best a big gleaming spinto soprano...."

## ATTILA:

In 1981, when Beverly Sills succeeded Julius Rudel as Director of the New York City Opera, her first new production was an early Verdi opera, *Attila*, which to date had never been performed in the United States. 28 years later, *Attila* was finally added to the Metropolitan Opera's schedule and was performed during its 2009-10 Season.

Back then, it felt like a grand homecoming to be singing the Italian operatic repertoire again after having most recently sung Wagner's *The Flying Dutchman* and *Die Meistersinger*. Which operas do I love to sing most? I just love to sing, period! When I sing the thing I am singing -- I love the thing I sing! Verdi and Wagner's music can enchant both the listener and performer alike. Verdi's *Attila* is full of loving lyricism and also difficult vocal acrobatics known as coloratura. One passage demanded that I sing as many as 20 different notes in one measure (the space in the music between the two vertical lines) within a count of only four beats. If you can manage to clear these vocal hurdles like a show horse at full gallop, then the opera *Attila* is for you.

*Attila* was one of Verdi's first operas. The main character in the opera is the King of a warlike band of Asiatic Nomads known as the Huns, who invaded and ravaged most of Europe. Their reason for doing so stemmed from their worship of the heathen warrior god, Odin. They killed, pillaged and maimed in his name. Contrary to Attila's orders, "To save no one!" a band of enemy women warriors are saved from death because they so gallantly took part in the fight against Attila that, instead of being killed, they are taken prisoner and offered to the King as a prize. I, as Odabella am their leader. I swear an angry oath of revenge, when I find that Attila had just killed my adored father, the Lord of Aquilea. Because I fearlessly led the women against Attila in battle, Attila feels a strange stirring of love for me and grants me one wish. I ask him for my sword back. He answers, "Here take mine instead." I sing my secret thoughts as if to myself, "Ah, a sword! O sublime, divine justice by you is now granted me. You have armed the hatred of the oppressed with the oppressor's sword. Pitiless steel, can you guess for whose breast your point is destined? The hour of vengence is at hand --- the Lord has revealed it."

There are also many subplots to be considered. One of them concerns my being in love with Foresto, an Aquileian Knight. He returns the emotion in equal portion. My main, never to be forgotten, objective in life, is, however, to avenge my father's death. Attila, being King, can make his own unbreakable rules. He decides to take me as his wife, making Foresto both jealous and angry.

**Odabella - "Attila"**
**New York City Opera**
**Los Angeles (1982)**

Odabella becomes aware of the fact that Foresto and Attila's enemies have concocted a poisonous draught in order to permanently rid the world of Attila. As Attila unwitingly lifts the cup of poison to his lips, I rush to warn him of his possible fate, not out of love but because of my determination to repay him in kind, with his own sword, for his cruelly taking my beloved father's life. Foresto quickly jockeys himself into position to stab Attila first, but I beat him to it and complete the task. As I stab him, I cry out, "Father! ---

Oh Father, I sacrifice him to you." I then turn and embrace my beloved Foresto as Attila sinks, realistically, to the stage floor murmuring, "You too, Odabella?" The curtain slowly closed but my colleague Samuel Ramey, who had brilliantly sung the role of Attila with rich sentorian tones, does not move. Stagehands rushed from the wings to help him up and make sure he was all right. As they raised him to my eye level and our eyes met, he said in a quivering voice from his tortured, grimacing lips, "Didn't anyone show you how to stab someone on stage? You should have placed the knife between my arm and my chest, not in my chest!" I apologized profusely for my ignorance and he managed a faint smile and a gentle pat of forgiveness on my cheek as he was helped off stage. Luckily the point of the sword had been purposely blunted long in advance of its use.

Several years later at a luncheon in New York given by the National Association of Singing Teachers, Samuel Ramey was honored. After a flowery introduction, he made his way to the podium. The first words out of his mouth were, "Before I talk about myself, I would like to acknowledge the presence of a highly regarded singer and colleague of mine -- Betty Jones! Please stand Betty." I was surprised and pleased, rising and bowing as he and the audience loudly clapped for me. I could now lay to rest forever my on going guilt regarding the sword stabbing fiasco. All obviously had been forgiven and forgotten.

# Oberon

In 1824, Carl Maria von Weber was invited by Covent Garden to compose the music for an opera, _Oberon,_ to be sung in English, and then to come to London the following season to conduct it. In order to compose "Oberon" for the British audience, von Weber, whose native tongue was German, intensively studied English. He could then better collaborate with the librettist, James Robinson Planche. Since von Weber was suffering from the final stages of tuberculosis, this was to be his last opera. It contains some of his greatest music. The collaboration with Planche proved frustratingly unsuccessful and produced a ludicrous libretto, thereby preventing the opera from taking the place in the repertory that its musical qualities merited. Many attempts were made to revive or improve the libretto but they succeeded only in making matters worse. In one of the many letters von Weber wrote to Planche, he complained, "The mixing of so many principal non-singing actors and the omission of music from its most important moments, -- deprives our _Oberon_ from being a true opera and will make it unfit to be performed in all the theaters of Europe."

_Oberon_'s best qualities were musical rather than dramatic, so it easily lent itself to concert performances. My new management, Eric Semon Inc., was told that a concert performance was scheduled to take place at Carnegie Hall the following February. An audition was quickly set up for me with the brilliant Eve Queler, one of the few female conductors in the country at the time. She had already made a strong impact on classical music by establishing the Opera Orchestra of New York and excelled at bringing rarely heard music to the public for its edification and enjoyment. I felt her welcoming warmth as soon as I met her. My audition proved to be a success and I was engaged as the "cover" for Roberta Knie, who had already been selected to sing the leading female role of Rezia.

Eve Queler made sure that I was well rehearsed in the role. I enjoyed working with her because she was so thorough. Her wise foresight meant we avoided many problems. A full rehearsal with the orchestra and singers was held before a small audience at the Pace University Auditorium located adjacent to New York's City Hall. I was pleased to be given the opportunity to sing this performance, as the designated cover, for it augmented my understanding of the role of Rezia.

von Weber's _Oberon_ marked the beginning of German classical music's romantic era. Wagner followed in his footsteps by continuing to further develop the many musical ideas which were first broached by von Weber. One aria Rezia sings is quite Wagneresque and difficult. It spans a two octave range from high "C" to middle "C." In the story, Oberon, the Elf King, has quarreled with his wife and decided not to see her again. They are to be reconciled only when he finds a pair of faithful lovers. He chooses Sir Huon, a bachelor Knight, and Rezia as a test couple. Through magic, Oberon causes them to undergo a shipwreck, be captured by pirates, be forced into slavery, and sentenced to death before he finally intervenes to save them. The couple's faithfulness to each other never wavers. Oberon praises them as examples of unshakable fidelity, and all ends well when he returns to his wife as promised.

The plot dictates how opera music must ultimately be composed. In one scene, Rezia and Fatima, her servant, overlook the ocean. Rezia searches the horizon for the arrival of a boat that will rescue them. Her aria is the heaviest and most demanding I was to perform in my entire operatic career. It is called "Ozean, du Ungeheuer!" or, translated into English, "Ocean, thou mighty monster." The aria is quite long and there are many rhythmic changes that keep the audience on the edge of their seats. In some sections the orchestra strikes a chord and holds it and then is completely silent, giving the singer a chance to express herself dramatically and for emphasis take liberties with the rhythms. The conductor may even hold the baton perfectly still but must be prepared in split second timing to continue. Since this aria describes the many moods of the ocean, the singer must know the technique of stressing certain words for further emphasis. When the ocean is described as stormy, the singer must breathe in very deeply from the diaphragm and honor the composer's directive, flexing the abs as hard as possible. It resembles doing a sit up from a lying position, so as to be able to make certain syllables louder than others. I rely on this technique when I am called upon to sing the more dramatic sections of this opera. As an aside, the reason the costumes for divas are made with high waistlines is to hide all the rippling muscular action when producing these declamative tones.

Getting back to the story, Rezia is overjoyed to see a boat at last on the ocean's horizon. It is Huon, her love, coming to rescue her at last. Although fate has temporarily separated them, they have remained constant and faithful to each other throughout. Oberon accepts their example and decides to live the rest of his days happily with his once rejected wife.

The afternoon of the Carnegie Hall performance, I received a hurried call from the conductor, "Betty, --- Roberta Knie just called and cancelled. Please come to New York right away! You will have to go on for her." I thanked Eve Queler, hung up the phone and lost no time in packing my concert dress and shoes when the phone rang again. This time it was Doug calling from Florida, where he was visiting his Fort Lauderdale Office, "Hi Sweetie Pie! --- what are you doing?" he asked. "I'm getting myself together to drive to New York. I'm singing _Oberon_ at Carnegie Hall tonight," I answered excitedly. As he continued, Doug sounded more and more like he had broken into a cold sweat when he quickly questioned, "But, --- you don't know it!" I countered defiantly with a smothered giggle, "I will by tonight! I have to go now Doug. I'll call you later and let you know how it all went. OK? Wish me luck!"

When I arrived at Carnegie Hall and had parked my car, I went straight to the stage where chairs had already been placed facing the quiet, darkened hall. I chose one and sat down to begin the process of gradual relaxation. The longer I sat in silence, the more at home I felt. A wished for peace began to wash over me, freeing me to center my consciousness on the hundred and one things I must deal with when performing and not let negative fear interrupt my positive inner communication. When I felt equal to the task ahead of me, I retired to my dressing room to touch up my make up, put on my concert gown and shoes, and peruse the score for the last time.

A knock on the door alerted me to the fact that I was wanted on stage. When I arrived, the conductor Eve Queler, was in the midst of verbally tying up the last minute loose ends before curtain time. My smiling colleagues greeted me and each other with warm emotionally supportive hugs and handshakes. Eve made her way directly to me and asked, "Betty do you think you know the score well enough to sing it tonight from memory?" I told her "No --- I'm afraid that I don't feel secure enough to do that." Eve immediately turned and announced to the whole cast, "Well then, all singers will also use their scores on stage during the performance, even those who have sung it before and don't need the score."

There is a special sacrosanct bond that encircles singers who are performing together. This magical evening, I was to sing on stage at Carnegie Hall with internationally known artists from the Metropolitan Opera. One such person was the world famous tenor Nicolai Gedda, who was to sing the role of Huon, Rezia's beloved knight. During all the pre-concert rehearsals he had been especially friendly and helpful to me, the novice. The opera originally sung in English, had been

translated into German, the language of the version I was to
sing. Our performance before a sold out audience went off
without a hitch and, judging from the applause, was enjoyed
by all. Afterwards the cast formed a receiving line to greet
the jubilant audience members. I thanked each one in turn
for coming and for the many positive comments they made as
they shook my hand and passed on to greet the other
performers. To my surprise, a group of people greeted me in
German. They enthusiastically bubbled on until I said, "I'm
sorry. I sing in German but unfortunately I don't speak it
fluently." One embarrassed member of the group said in
English with a heavy accent, "Oh! we're from the German
Embassy. The way you sang Rezia, --- we thought you were
German too. Congratulations! You were wonderful."

The next day the reviewers from the most read New York
newspapers summed up their views of the performance.
Harriet Johnson of the New York Post wrote:

> "....As soprano Roberta Knie became ill with the flu,
> Betty Jones who had been her understudy, sang the
> role of Rezia. Miss Jones possesses a fine rich
> soprano...."

Harold Schomberg of the New York Times said:

> "....She did get a good hand for 'Ozean, du
> Ungeheuer'. The third act Cavatina gave her a lyric
> line to exploit and this she did with style and
> charm...."

Bill Zakariasen said of me in his New York Daily News
review:

> "....The performance was generally fine giving an
> excellent case for a work far more worth knowing
> beyond the familiar Overture and the grueling
> soprano aria, 'Ocean, thou mighty Monster'. That aria

and the rest of Rezia were ably sung by Betty Jones, a last minute replacement for the flu-fallen Roberta Knie...."

The New Yorker Magazine printed in its music review:

"....Rezia was sung by Betty Jones replacing Roberta Knie. She was secure and powerful, a sound musician and a reliable singer...."

And last, an article in Connecticut's Sunday Post read:

"....Justine and John Macurdy (he is the Metropolitan Opera basso from Stamford) report that they heard Eve Queler conduct the Opera Orchestra in New York in Oberon at Carnegie Hall, and Wilton's opera soprano, Betty Jones was the substitute for the announced soloist. She sang beautifully "Best I have ever heard her" reported Justine who is herself an opera coach...."

Two days after my Carnegie Hall performance, as I was packing to leave for Weisbaden, Germany to resume _Tosca_ rehearsals, Marianne Semon from my management called to say that various members of the Metropolitan Opera attended my _Oberon_ performance and they had offered me a contract to cover Leonie Rysanek as the Empress in their new production of _Die Frau Ohne Schatten._ She also mentioned that Karl Bohm, one of the greatest conductors of the 20th century and a major interpreter of _Die Frau_'s composer Richard Strauss, was the scheduled conductor.

## TWENTY EIGHT YEARS LATER:
The _Oberon_ experience took place the night of February 23, 1978, when I was called to sing unexpectedly on five hours notice. Years later, in March 2005, my telephone in Wilton, Connecticut rang. I picked it up and said, "Hello?" One of my current voice students, Mary Jane Fast, replied hurriedly,

"Betty, I've just received an e-mail from a man in Germany asking about you. He's been looking for you all over the internet world and finally connected when he saw on my website that you were my voice teacher. He desperately wants to get in touch with you. May I have your permission to give him your e-mail address?" I answered, "Oh sure. I wonder what this is all about. Thanks, Mary Jane."

That same day, I received an e-mail from a Thomas Tillman in Germany. He said, "I have just heard a recently released CD of a live recording of _Oberon_ in which you sang gloriously. I was totally enchanted by the way you handled the role of Rezia and the very difficult Ozean aria." He then said that he would be writing a review of the new recording and with my permission would like to write "A portrait of Betty Jones" for an on-line Musik Magazine. "There are so many questions I'd like to ask you. I will also make sure that the recording company sends you some of the new _Oberon_ CD's. Before e-mailing him back, I mulled over a few questions which gnawed constantly at my innards. First of all, during the rehearsals and performance I never heard any whispers about the possibility of a recording being made. No permission had been requested of me and no contracts signed. I thought to myself this could be a pirate recording. Someone must have had the latest equipment and recorded the entire concert performance live. In spite of my trepidations, I accepted the request from Tillman. Sure enough, there arrived shortly by mail five CD's. I was overwhelmed to hear myself for the first time sing accompanied by a full symphony orchestra. Almost 30 years had elapsed since the performance, yet this CD was being sold all over the world as though the performance had just occurred.

Thomas Tillman and I e-mailed furiously back & forth until he felt he had gleaned enough information about me to write his article. After it was published, he sent me a copy. My curiorsity was completely thwarted when I realized that I was unable to understand most of it as it was written completely in German. I discussed my predicament with one of my voice students who, fluent in this language, offered to translate it into English. She returned at her appointed time the next week to take her lesson with me and presented me with the finished work. After she left, I kicked off my shoes and curled up on the living room couch to savor this special moment of joy alone with the manuscript. It was entitled: Betty Jones, An Entertainer Who Can Also Sing Opera. A portrait of Oberon's "Rezia" performed on February 23, 1978 at New York's Carnegie Hall by Thomas Tillmann, English Translation by Lilian Revel March 2005. The eight page article figuratively took me by the hand and led me back through time, calling to mind the many pleasurable musical high points of my life. After first reading, I snuggled deeper into the soft couch and began to ruminate on the attendant circumstances which brought it into being. What completely stymied me was that, among all the millions of people on this earth, Thomas Tillman was, thanks to computer technology, able to search me out. My good fortune was mind boggling. Except for the intervention of fate, I would never have known about the _Oberon_ CD.

## Betty Jones: An Entertainer Who Can Also Sing Opera

**A Portrait of *Oberon's* *"Rezia"* - performed on February 23, 1978 at New York's Carnegie Hall**

by Thomas Tillmann, *English Translation by Lilian Revel*
March 2005

"Small world, isn't it?" argues Mama Rose in the famous musical *Gypsy*. This phrase was going through my mind when I recently received an e-mail from the American singer, Mary Jane Southouse Fast. I had searched Mary Jane's homepage and left her a message when I was trying to find biographical information concerning the soprano, Betty Jones. On a recently released CD of a live recording of Von Weber's *OBERON* (see our review of the CD published by Mitridate), Betty Jones sings an explosive "Rezia" and I had not been able to find anything about this singer in the usual reference manuals. Mary Jane answered my inquiry by explaining that she had been a voice student of Betty Jones, and that she would refer my request directly to her teacher. And a few days later, I heard from Betty Jones, who by substituting for an indisposed Roberta Knie, had indeed saved that *OBERON* performance at Carnegie Hall 27 years ago. This artist, who is now 75 years old and proud of it, recently celebrated her 50th wedding anniversary. Betty has two children -- son Jeff, who has his own sound studio in New York City and deals mainly with jazz musicians; and daughter Janet, who also studied music and dance, but now works in a high position for a worldwide commodities trading firm -- and three grandchildren. She nevertheless does not lead the typical contemplative life of a grandmother, but is much sought after as a superb voice teacher and still continues to include operatic arias during concert appearances.

Betty Jones (left) and the Pianist Sally Bailey (right) in January 2005

At the time of the *OBERON* performance, Betty Jones was the official "cover" for Roberta Knie. Five hours before curtain call on February 23, 1978, the telephone rang in Betty's house: Roberta Knie had to cancel at the last minute due to a sudden indisposition. As the experienced "cover" she was, Betty immediately left her home in Wilton, Connecticut, and drove her own car to New York, a distance of about 50 miles. (Her husband was on a business trip in Florida and couldn't make it to the concert in time, the couple emotionally told me. By listening to the recently released CD, he was finally able to hear his wife's triumphant performance for the first time). When Betty arrived at Carnegie Hall, she sat down on the still darkened stage and tried to concentrate as much as possible. She fully realized that the attention of the opera loving audience was not going to be directed only to the Metropolitan Opera star tenor, Nicolai Gedda, but also on the relatively unknown soprano who would be singing the famous aria, "Ocean, thou mighty monster". (Gedda by the way was very nice to her and couldn't believe that she had never sung the role of Rezia before - nor could anyone else). She remembers Eve Queler asking if "I knew the role well enough to sing without the music?" Due to my limited knowledge of German, I immediately said no upon which she ordered all the singers on stage to use their scores.

After the concert, there was a big reception. Betty Jones remembers being greeted by guests from the German Embassy who were astonished to find out that she wasn't fluent in German, but was nevertheless able to sing and be fully understood in this language. Also in the audience were many members of the Metropolitan Opera. "The next morning my manager called to say that I had been offered a 'Met' contract to cover the 'Empress' in *Die Frau Ohne Schatten*." The fact that Leonie Rysanck didn't get sick, and that Betty could thus not perform did not upset her. She is grateful for everything her career has granted her and does not regret what didn't come to pass.

Nevertheless, reviewers had been given a chance to notice her. "She possesses an excellent, very promising and rich soprano voice" said Harriett Johnson of the New York Post, who had also heard a few technical flaws. The famous Harold C. Schonberg didn't only have a problem with her name -- he called her "Betsy" -- but he found her interpretation too forced and uneven, although he could not dismiss the tremendous applause after the feared "Ocean" aria. He did acknowledge, however, her style and charm as the lyrical vocal lines of the "Cavatina" in the third act developed. Other reviewers found her singing very sure and strong and called her an excellent musician, a reliable singer and an expressive interpreter.

Betty Jones, the Rezia in Oberon-Performed at New York's Carnegie Hall

But who was this Betty Jones, who on the afternoon of February 23, 1978, was only known to a few insiders; and who, on the morning of February 24th, the entire opera world in New York was talking about with astonishment and admiration!

A big singing career was not part of her upbringing, even though Betty Jones remembers that singing had always been a part of her being and that she always sang for herself and for others. She attended Sarah Lawrence College and majored in art (graduating in 1951). Although she was part of and sang in the "Double Quartet" while in college, Betty did not have any extensive voice training as one would need for a career in opera. "At the beginning, I didn't even know how to read music or play the piano. Every single note needed to be taught to me by a coach."

# Other Performances

## PORGY AND BESS:

I fell in love with George Gershwin's _Porgy and Bess_ when I sang the role of Bess in a semi-staged production at Sarah Lawrence College. His music can be very operatic, yet retain the flavor of its Broadway beginnings, and is further spiced by the hypnotic rhythms borrowed from black culture. I also felt privileged to have experienced a special family connection with Gershwin. My father's sister, Gladys, shared with me that, "Back in the 30's, our friend George Gershwin came to our apartment and played excerpts from his newly composed folk opera, _Porgy and Bess_. We absolutely loved it!" Aunt Gladys was married to Walter White, the head of the NAACP, and they lived at 409 Edgecomb Avenue, a prestigious address in Harlem, where former Supreme Court Justice, Thurgood Marshall also lived.

I owe the Wilton Playshop much kudos for including in a benefit during the early 1960's the famous love duet "Bess, You Is my Woman Now," which I sang along with a local black baritone, James Young. Jim sang with such warmth and finesse that I wondered jealously at the time how I, too, could also possess this inscrutable secret of expressiveness. It was not until I became privy to his past musical credits that I found the answer. He had been soloist with the Depaw Infantry Chorus when in the US Army during World War II, sang in the Broadway Musical _Call Me Mister_ and in Virgil Thompson's all black opera _Four Saints in Three Acts_. I pondered these events and came to the conclusion that, as the old bromide states, "Experience is the best teacher."

Unknown to me, it seemed that fate was clearing a path for me to sing excerpts from _Porgy and Bess_ in a local concert. George Gershwin's sister Francis Gershwin Godowsky lived in Westport, Connecticut and heard about my singing

177

through my accompanist Don Comrie, who had been asked
to play in the performance. She made up her mind then and
there to engage me to sing at the open air Levitt Pavilion,
where on a summer's evening, after eating your home made
picnic dinner and sitting on a blanket under a starry sky, one
could hear a free concert performed on a brightly lit
professional stage near the bubbling Saugatuck River.
Abraham Lind-Oquendo, a New Yorker, lent his beautiful
baritone voice and professional expertise to the music of the
cripple, Porgy. More than any other cast member, he really
knew what he was doing because he had sung the role of
Porgy many times on Broadway. Doug both narrated this
performance and sang the role of the overbearing cruel
character Crown. Although Doug had never studied voice, his
is naturally gifted. His body's resonating chambers (sinuses,
large chest cavity, etc.) give him an impressive speaking voice
and also an exceptional singing voice as well. An inter-racial
group called the Serendipity Chorale directed by Gigi
VanDyke, who would soon become my daughter's mother-in-
law, ably sang the choral music.

There is a pleasurable soul satisfaction in singing or just
hearing Gershwin's spiritually inspiring music. Here we find a
plethora of entreatingly sung prayers which can be
emotionally supportive. Drive through New York's Harlem
today and note the number of churches on any given block.
During a service on a given Sunday, hear the singing with
abandon and the clapping that seeps out from under the
doors and windows. Gershwin caught that spark and his
music fanned it into a bright flame.

## PORGY AND BESS CONCERT:
Around this time my concert career singing _Porgy and Bess_
took off, carrying me up like superman to unexpected
heights. A new version of the opera entitled "_Porgy & Bess
Concert_" was arranged for voice, chorus, orchestra or piano by
Robert Russell Bennett and made its advent into the public's
eye and ear. The smaller roles had been deleted but all their

important solos were awarded to either Porgy or Bess. Every segue (the music between the arias) was filled with music that could modulate into different keys as needed. This version was only 45 minutes long and could easily fill one act of a concert. The new arrangement caught on like a California wild fire and was just what I was looking for. Symphony Orchestras immediately added it to their repertoire, placing me in a position of great demand both at home and abroad. I was engaged to sing this fabulous vehicle with numerous symphony orchestras, including the San Diego, Anchorage, Alaska, Jacksonville, Norwalk, Buffalo Philharmonic, Brevard, etc.

Franz Allers, a conductor at the Metropolitan Opera, was scheduled to conduct the Chicago Symphony's performance. A Met soprano was almost signed to sing it when Allers decided to engage me instead after my audition. The performance must have cast a magical spell over both the audience and conductor because, whenever Allers was asked to conduct the 45 minute version of Porgy again, he made sure that Betty Jones was there to sing Bess. His intervention made it possible for me to further recreate the role with the St Louis Symphony, Milwaukee Symphony and others.

I also became further known because of the helpful insights I shared with the other performers. When I sang in Chicago, the usually black chorus was racially all white. After they sang "I ain't got no shame" in rehearsal, I volunteered a helpful critique. Under the baton of the choral conductor Margaret Hillis, the singing seemed to lack a core, method acting reason for existence. I volunteered advice, "When you sing this piece you have to pretend that your straight laced great aunt has just startled you by flinging your closet door wide open, catching you as you sit on your father's shoes on the floor doing pleasurable naughties on yourself. You spring up and sing both loudly and saucily, "I aint got no shame doing what I like to do; Sun ain't got no shame; Moon aint got no shame so I ain't got no shame doing what I like to do." This insight literally added purpose and color to the song, making it a toe tapping, applause worthy piece.

## PORGY AND BESS IN SWEDEN AND ENGLAND:

In 1983, I was ceremoniously welcomed in Stockholm, Sweden and Bournemouth, England, where I lent my singing talent to an even longer, more complete concert version of the opera. By this time I was 53 years old and was pleasantly surprised to be engaged to sing the role of Serena. Her tour de force is the dramatic aria "My Man's Gone Now," which calls for a richer, darker and stronger vocal timbre than Bess. In song she pitifully bewails her sorrow at the loss of her beloved husband, making good use of an expansive vocal range.

When I sang this role in Sweden, the other major roles were all sung by American Blacks. We were accompanied by the Swedish Radio Symphony and Chorus. Some of the small roles were sung or spoken by local white Swedish singers and actors. One such role was that of a detective who questions Serena about Crown's murder. My almost overwhelming problem was trying to keep a straight face when, with an all but unintelligibly heavy Swedish accent, the detective spoke his lines in English. "Come on down Serena Robbins! Do you mean to tell me that Crown was murdered right outside your window and you didn't know it?"

**"Porgy and Bess" Concert Tour**
**Sweden & England (1983)**

It seemed that the entire orchestra had thought, for some unknown reason, that this performance would likely be cancelled, so they had not studied the music and rehearsed as they should have. We were told that, because of the lack of preparation, a section of the music that called for a delightfully percussive banjo solo would have to be skipped. During our first rehearsal, our American conductor, Harold Farberman, had to take over the playing of the drums and show the local drummer how to play the complicated syncopated rhythms of African origin that usher in the character Sporting Life's famous, "It Ain't Necessarily So." Nevertheless, we all pulled together as a group and, because of our sincere communal efforts, our performance was a success and elicited a commensurate applause. I learned during this period that one cannot count on anything for sure! Be as prepared as possible and if the worst happens --- roll with the punch.

My last concert version of *Porgy and Bess* was sung in Bournemouth, on the southern coast of England, an elegant and delightful resort town whose main park boasts of huge, live green palm trees. We hoped the Bournemouth Symphony Orchestra, known internationally for its excellent recordings, would provide a solid support for our vocal flights of fancy. I have always thought of the English as culturally conservative, evidenced by the purity of the English language they bequeathed us.

In Stockholm, I found it to be disconcerting, when singing on the stage before an audience, to hear sections of the Swedish Radio Symphony totter and stumble along. Here, from the moment the Bournemouth Symphony plunged into the spirited, fast overture until the last boogiefully impressive finale, the orchestra delivered Gershwin's ideas unaltered, from his great mind directly to our ears, while preaching a tuneful sermon of hope and farewell.

> "Oh Lawd, I'm on my way
> I'm on my way to the Heav'nly Lan'
> I'll ride dat long, long road
> If you are there to guide my han'
>
> Oh Lawd, I'm on my way
> I'm on my way to the Heav'nly Lan'
> Oh Lawd, its a long, long way
> but you'll be there to take my han'

## CONCERTS IN GERMANY:

Thanks to the accompanist, Shirley Seguin, I was made privy to some upcoming opera concerts in Germany. Managers generally know what is transpiring job wise in the world of music and pass the information to the artists on their roster so they will build bigger careers and the manager will eventually collect larger commissions. Accompanists, on the other hand, also hear about the current musical opportunities, sometimes directly from their colleagues or the artists for whom they play. Their motives are usually altruistic and not primarily monetary.

One afternoon in 1979, while I was working with Shirley at her New York studio, she suddenly stopped playing and seemed to be lost in thought. "Shirley," I asked gently, "Is there something the matter?" "Oh no" she exclaimed. "Just thinking --- I was helping William Wilderman brush up an aria he was preparing to sing soon when he told me he's been searching high and low for just the right soprano to concertize with him in Germany." "Do you know of anyone?" he questioned. "If it's alright with you Betty," Shirley confided, "I'd like to give him your name and number. I think your voices would sound marvelous on stage together." With joyful expectancy, I purred, "It definitely would give me great pleasure to appear with him." Shirley continued, "Lets make a date then when Willi can hear you." My heart skipped a beat when I realized the glorious prospect of meeting and singing with a 25 year veteran performer from the Metropolitan Opera.

At our first meeting, I felt very comfortable with Willi. He was tall and trim with well kept graying hair and a stylishly clipped beard to match. There was something about his personality that reminded me very much of my father. They were both conservative, inner directed and would laugh uncontrollably when enjoying a good joke. After a successful audition and the dates, time and places of the concerts shared, Doug hurriedly made my last minute travel arrangements.

Concert Tour
Germany (1985)

Germany in the late fall can be quite cold, so I wore my almost floor length racoon coat to greet the welcoming emissaries at the Stuttgart Airport, who touchingly presented me with a large, multi-colored floral bouquet. I was then driven from the airport to the home of Anneliese and Gerhart Schnapper in Baltmannsweiler. When I arrived, a little travel weary, the Schnappers only thought was to make me feel more comfortable as soon as possible. They vacated their own bedroom and gave it over to my use, knowing that Doug soon would be arriving to attend the concerts and that we would want to be together. They treated me like family! When I was cold, they turned up the heat, which they normally did only when their grandchildren were visiting. I could toast marshmallows on the emotional warmth which bubbled up from the hearts of many of the people I met. During rehearsals, Willi solved the enigma --- "They are all my relatives Betty. Baltmannsweiler was my hometown before moving to America." By sharing this information with me, he symbolically fitted into place the last missing piece in this loving family's puzzle.

It was very gratifying to at last meet the conductor, Eugen Mayer, and begin rehearsals. The conductor must have been rehearsing the chorus and orchestra for some time, considering how well they played and sang the music. Members of the chorus and orchestra all lived in the neighboring towns and knew each other. As soloist, I was responsible for singing some vocally very difficult music including Leonora's aria from

**Stuttgart Airport, Germany (1979)**

Beethoven's _Fidelio,_ Senta's ballad from Wagner's _The Flying Dutchman_ and three scenes from Verdi's _La Forza del Destino_ (not in Italian but in German). Willi Wilderman sang the bass arias from all of these demanding operas, which were relieved by lighter fare here and there. During rehearsal breaks, we were all invited to sip ice cold amber colored beer, socialize and eat steaming hot knockwurst spread with yellow mustard. Resuming our work again after the welcomed rest, we felt much more refreshed, satisfied and ready to plough ahead.

Our first concert took place on October 20, 1979 in the sold out Metzinger Concert Hall, where I received a good review from the local newspaper the next day.

"......Soprano Betty Jones who possesses enormous vocal resources and whose dark timbre resembles more that of a mezzo, interpreted Beethoven's Leonore's recitative and aria from _Fidelio_ which was quite impressive and          dramatically moving. Full of passion, she sang Senta's ballad from Wagner's _Flying Dutchman_ and also  the solo with choir sections of Verdi's _La Forza del Destino._ She fascinated everyone with her strong and variable voice. Willi Wilderman distinguished himself too. He gave Darland's aria from The _Flying Dutchman_ the most beautiful expression. In the Verdi and Lortzing duets, he and Betty Jones joined in exquisite harmony....."

We repeated the same concert the following week in the neighboring town of Esslingen at their Stadhalle (Concert Hall). A new review stated:

".....Betty Jones has a remarkable fully developed dramatic soprano voice with coloratura capabilities which she uses to paint   rich and varied pictures of expressions without any hesitation in the various registers nor holding back in the high and most exposed regions; a voice that can equally plead, mourn, triumph and shine on this occasion enraptured  the sold out house......"

Five years after these concerts, Willi Wilderman and I were invited back again to perform a similar program in both Metzinger and Esslingen. These performances took place in March 1985.

## SINGING FOR HOSPICE:

Ella Grasso Awards
Connecticut Hospice
Branford, CT. (1991)

Doug was asked to join the Hospice of Connecticut Board and soon became its Vice Chairman. This organization, dedicated to the compassionate end-of-life movement, started in New Haven, Connecticut and has since spread worldwide. In order to qualify as a Hospice patient, your doctor must medically evaluate you and decide that your chances of further survival are slim and all extraordinary life support procedures should be terminated. Philosophically, Hospice centers its attention on their patients maintaining, under dire circumstances, the best level of health and happiness possible to the end.

It quickly became known that the new Vice Chairman's wife, Betty Jones, was an opera singer. The Executive Director asked Doug if I would consider singing at a Hospice Annual Awards Program. I was delighted to have the opportunity to help in any way I could. By word of mouth, I found out that a member of their staff, Sally Bailey, an ordained minister, whose job it was to tend to the spiritual needs of the dying, was also a first class accompanist. Unknown to me, she had already volunteered to accompany me during the program.

Betty Jones

I searched through my music thoroughly and put together a program filled with poetic word pictures and uplifting thoughts, interspersed with downright knee slapping, toe tapping tunes and humor. I used the power of music to give my precious audience a much needed vacation from their pain, worry and fear. My heart filled to the brim with joy when I saw, in reaction to my performance, smiles bloom forth from the faces of all present.

**WILTON LIBRARY:**
As part of the Wilton Library's Centennial Year Celebration, I was asked to present the closing program of the series on Sunday Afternoon, December 10, 1995, lovingly entitled "A Bouquet to Wilton." I included arias, spirituals, show tunes and amusing moments from my singing career, which was born and encouraged to grow in my adopted home town, Wilton.

The Candlelight Concert Series, one of the better known concert programs, was also sponsored by the Wilton Library. In 1972, I was the first singer ever asked to appear. Until then they had featured only instrumentalists. Although most of the artists who performed these musical events lived locally, they all had previously performed nationally or internationally at some point in their careers and had accumulated an elite following.

188

Dec. 6, 1995 Bulletin, Wilton, Conn.

# Betty Jones's concert Sunday is her 'Bouquet to Wilton'

**Concert - Wilton Library**
**Wilton, CT. (1995)**

## <u>UNIVERSITY OF BRIDGEPORT</u>:

In the early 60's, long before I even thought about a career in opera, we got to know conductor/composer Leonard Bernstein and his family. They had a home near us in Connecticut which to this day his daughter Nina still occupies.

Fast forward several years to when I was teaching voice at the University of Bridgeport and was asked to be one of the featured artists at their gala music faculty concert. Although not a faculty member, the famous Bernstein was also scheduled to appear. Looking forward with glowing anticipation to the renewal of our casual friendship, I decided to sing some of his composed songs. The concert proved to be a resounding success. At the end, when the last strains of

189

music and applause had died down,  the audience rose to depart. Bernstein, with his arms flung wide, smilingly rushed to greet and embrace me.  He effervesced positive critiques with regard to my performance of his music but then gently shared a few almost inaudible negative thoughts about the questionable artistry of my accompanist. His one concern was that curious bystanders would somehow be able to hear his comments, possibly by reading his lips, so he pursed them and signaled me to do the same. Like two still lipped ventriloquists we conversed at length.  A photographer stealthily crept up then asked our permission to snap our picture but as to our conversation, thank goodness, no one was the wiser.

**With Leonard Bernstein**
**Bridgeport University Concert**

# Opera Antics

**"Opera Antics" Performance (1998)**

When it finally came time for me to retire from the professional opera stage, I returned to an art form I had yearned to share again with audiences as I had in the past. Humor, missing from my performing life for far too long, made a glorious re-entry into my repertoire. Usually the plots and sub plots of grand opera are filled with unrequited love, murder or suicide brought to the fore by relentless feelings of retribution, fear, duty and guilt in the hearts of the lead characters. What kind of music would make me the happiest to perform at this time in my life? After giving it some thought, I decided that arias from opera, classical art songs, jazz and Broadway tunes in a show knitted together with insights and laughs, would bring me the greatest joy. Thus *OperaAntics* was born. The format of the show was to be totally malleable and no two shows needed ever be exactly alike. I always took into consideration the age, education and ethnic background of each audience, creating shows that would movingly touch their hearts, minds and funny bones.

On Saturday Evening, December 12, 1987 I first performed the new *OperaAntics* Program for The Fine Arts Society in the grand ballroom of the elite Ritz Carlton Hotel in Naples, Florida. The Naples Daily News reviewed my performance in an article entitled, "Christmas at the Ritz." It said;

"….Soprano Betty Jones, who appeared in a Fine Arts *Porgy and Bess* concert last year, once again held the capacity audience en-thralled with her one-woman show *OperaAntics*. Her program ranged from Verdi, Wagner, Bernstein and Kurt Weil to a gossamer rendition of Gershwin's 'Summertime.' Jones weaves her eclectic program together with hilarious anecdotes about what it's like to be a 6 foot statuesque diva, singing love drenched arias with miniature tenors. She also told about hanging out with other Big Chick Valkyries. 'When we went out to eat together we made a formidable looking group. Head waiters scurried to find us the best tables in our favorite Intime restaurants,' she chuckled. While performing *Porgy and Bess* in Sweden she described the plight of the local Swedish singer's struggle to capture the cadence of the black American's southern dialect. "Fish are yumping' was as close as they could get. Jones takes her high spirited musical show to schools and also delights senior citizen groups with her beautiful singing and ebullient brand of showmanship…."

Experience has taught me that I can make it easier for audiences to understand what I am singing in a foreign language if I tell them  the plot and assume certain poses while translating the words. Then I repeat the poses while singing. After the show a congratulatory crowd usually encircles me. Many have been stunned that they could actually understand what my character was singing about. One volunteered, "I've never been to an opera before but your show has really piqued my interest. Which opera do you think I ought to hear first?"

Performing for grammar or high school students brings its own special brand of challenges. Most kids have never heard an adult operatic voice like mine before. Some have knitted their eyebrows together as I sang. A few have stuck their fingers in their ears to block out the unfamiliar sound, showing me immediately that young ears are very sensitive. A good choice of repertoire, however, can arouse their interest and save the day. To begin with, I would ask the audience, "How do cavemen call their buddies in the jungle?" Then I would do the Johnny Weissmuller Tarzan yell made famous by Comedian Carol Burnett. My accompanist would then play the main theme from *The Sound of Music* and I would ask, "How do you sing from one peak to another in the Swiss Alps?" Answering my own question I would don a faux metal hat with long blond braids attached and sing Wagner's Valkyrie whoop or yodeling. If it was near Christmas I would ask everyone to make believe that they were dogs and to help me bark "Jingle Bells" on pitch. Having won over their resistance, I would continue by singing songs written exclusively for children by A.A. Milne, who wrote *Winnie the Pooh,* or more current Broadway tunes. Saving my quieting favorite tune for last, I would favor the audience with "Over the Rainbow," from *The Wizard of Oz.*

On another occasion, I was engaged to sing a program for the students at Fairfield University in Connecticut. I had heard through the grapevine that those from the school's football team were less than pleased to find that they were expected to attend a concert to hear an opera singer sing as part of their course in music. They had been up late the night before dancing and cheering around a yellow bonfire at a football rally. When I entered the hall, I was not at all surprised to see most of those present slumped down in their chairs, some with the corners of their mouths turned down and eyes half closed. In reaction, I said to myself snidely, "I'm more than well prepared to deal with this situation! Look out everybody!"

A professor introduced me by recounting my more important artistic successes. Weak applause welcomed me as I took the stage, front and center. Hidden in the dark recesses of my pocket were a necklace and a five dollar bill. The beads of the necklace were given me by admirers when I sang _Porgy and Bess_ in Alaska. The Alaskans proudly use moose dropping to make this especially unique form of jewelry. As my accompanist took his place at the piano and readied his music, I reached into my pocket and withdrew my precious cachet. Holding both objects aloft, I questioned with a broad smile, "A five dollar bill goes to the first person who can tell me what this necklace is made of?" Their half mast eyelids instantly sprang wide open. The bodies of all reclining students slid quickly upright to the edge of their chairs, so that they could more closely appraise these two objects and quietly compare verbal notes with their nearest neighbor. One young man with a smug smile on his face suddenly sprang completely out of his chair and teetered on his toes. While waving his attention getting arms above his head, he shouted, "I know what it is! I know! --- It's SHIT!" "You're right," I yelled back. "The five dollars is yours." From this point on in my performance, I could do no wrong. After each selection they clapped, whistled and cheered like they must have done around the bonfire the night before.

After more than 200 performances of my one woman show both here in the United States and as far away as Australia, I realized that the promise I made to myself, "Know your audience," had paid off royally. I have given them what I thought they wanted in the language and repertoire that proved to please them. I sang to them in English, Italian, French, Spanish, German, Yiddish, Hebrew, Russian, Czechoslovakian and Chinese. They all had a jolly good time listening, participating and learning, while in reaction either laughing or sometimes sympathetically shedding a tear

**Betty Jones: One Woman Show**

# Teaching

Ever since I began to make more of a name for myself, both in the world of opera and on the concert stage, I was approached to share my expertise by teaching voice at The University of Bridgeport, Fairfield University and the Westport School of Music during the 1980's. As time permitted, I also began to teach privately at my Wilton home studio.

When a new student begins to study voice with me, I never know for sure where the slow process of vocal metamorphosis will lead. The outer shell of the oyster may just hide a precious vocal pearl of great beauty within. I always have rescuing jokes on the tip of my tongue, just in case fear rears its frightening head and disrupts a lesson. Laughter is a marvelous method of relaxation and helps to refocus the mind. Young school children studying with me replenish my store of funnies by bringing me their best clean jokes, which I either use judiciously or file away in my grey matter for future use. There is nothing magical or mysterious about singing, it obeys natures laws. A good technique can in time help produce an increasingly more beautiful sound as the muscles it incorporates become totally coordinated.

I have found that those students who have previously studied dance are the easiest to teach because they are already in touch with their bodies and can easily choreograph both small and large muscles at will. What is the best vocal exercise you can do to warm up the voice before singing? It is the yawn position! It opens the throat, lowers the larynx and prepares the best echo-tunnel chamber to enhance your sound. Add an open mouthed hum to give it a scintillating sound and you are in business. To attain richness in the higher register, repeatedly unhinge the jaw while singing like a python eating a pig. I wish I had a dollar for the millions of times I have asked my adult students over the years, "Open your mouth. Open Your Mouth! OPEN YOUR MOUTH!"

In order to pronounce your words clearly while keeping your mouth open in the high register, you must learn to become a ventriloquist. Tongue alone has to learn how to do all the work in producing open mouthed verbal clarity. Even to this day, when I go to the family dentist I enjoy talking with him while he is working in my mouth, the art of which I learned during my own voice lessons. The first time I did it, he seemed very unhappy and said, "Betty, you and I are having a jolly good time talking together. The only trouble is, I have a waiting room full of patients. As we talk, I'm finishing up my work in your mouth --- but they don't know that. All they hear is us enjoying a friendly conversation while they exasperatingly wait and wait and wait some more, hoping that they will soon be taken."

Diaphragmatic breathing is a must! I teach it by asking the student to lie down and place a book just above the belly button. I then ask them to push the book up towards the ceiling as they inhale. When they sing I also encourage singer hopefuls to make believe they have not defecated in a month of Sundays and to push down like they are relieving themselves as they sing. Their every note in the ascending scale demands an ever stronger support of this nature.

During public singing technique demonstrations, I have often invited an audience member to join me on stage and to punch me hard in my abdomen as I sustain a long steady high note. As long as I remain gut strong, my voice sings out without a hint of disturbance or waver. I do, however, caution my students, "to never eat beans before a performance or run the risk of unwanted fireworks at the wrong time."

Eight thousand people at the Spoleto Festival in Italy is the largest audience I have ever sung for, but it pleases me almost as much to demonstrate how to sing a troublesome musical passage for an audience of one during a lesson.

I also make sure that my teachable charges deliver the music as untouched as possible from the mind of the composer to the ear of the audience, while honoring all the directive markings and tempo changes. There is always a creative license in opera, which grants the possibility of imprinting your own unique artistic stamp on what you are singing. Knowledgeable artists can learn to safely navigate these two artistic poles, that of the composer and of the performer, blending them into one artistic amalgam.

# Special Family Remembrances

## BEING OUT ON THE WATER:

When Doug and I celebrated our honeymoon by sailing to Bermuda back in 1954, I soon learned what a serious boating enthusiast I had just married. From then on, being out on the water became an important part of our lives together. We left our land bound life on numerous occasions to sail all over the world on various cruise ships and freighters. We also frolicked locally on our motor yacht, the BETTY-GENE, which we enjoyed for over 30 years. It was docked just 15 minutes away from our Wilton, Connecticut home. Doug was the captain, I the first mate and our kitty "Nini" the second mate. Placed on board was a portable electronic piano which I used extensively to study and learn new opera roles while we were in port.

In 1974, honoring our 20th wedding anniversary, we took the entire family, including grandparents on another cruise to Bermuda. We returned there again on our 50th anniversary.

IN HONOR OF OUR

TWENTIETH ANNIVERSARY

MR. AND MRS. EUGENE D. JONES

CORDIALLY INVITE YOU

TO BE OUR GUEST

ON A

SEVEN DAY "SEA VENTURE" CRUISE

TO BERMUDA

DEPARTING NEW YORK AUGUST 31, 1974

R S V P

Wishing to further expand our sailing experiences, we were happy to learn that my manager was able to negotiate numerous lucrative shipboard singing engagements. The audiences on board welcomed with loud appreciative applause my choice of lighter show tunes counter balanced by more intricate and difficult operatic arias. For these gigs, I always brought my own accompanist and, on some occasions, Doug too. My accompanist proved to be an invaluable asset because many shipboard pianos were woefully out-of-tune. He always thought up ingenious ways to improve the tuning, including the use of swizzle sticks from the ship's bar to deaden errant strings. If during inclement weather, the ship rolled or pitched too much as I was performing, I learned to hold on to something strong and stationary or press my back against a load bearing column to steady myself. In every respect, we were always treated as honored guests not just employees of the shipping line. Doug loved these cruises the most because his only expense when it was all over, was the bar bill.

**Celebrating our 20th Wedding Anniversary (1974)**

Madelon, Doug and I cruising on the QE-2 (1998)
Madelon first introduced me to Doug in 1949

"Queensland Star" to Australia

**"Cast Otter" to Europe**

**"Kent Courier" to South America**

**Our beloved motor yacht BETTY-GENE**

Betty Jones

# Requiem for a second mate

To the Editors:

On Saturday, we lost our second mate to kidney failure; for her there is no dialysis for an unknown palpable mass and there was no operation.

Ninian Jones, affectionately known as Nini, was well into her middle years when she signed on as a crew member on the Betty-Gene docked at the Saugatuck Harbor Yacht Club in Westport, captained by Eugene Douglas and first mate, Betty Jones.

One of Nini's responsibilities was to make sure that the sun set in the west as ordered. She took her duties very seriously, surveying the process before twilight from the vantage point of the captain's helm. She kept her vigil until relieved by the moon and stars. Her yellow eyes could never understand why the green grass was always blue and why it rippled when making a slapping sound against the hull.

When the vessel was underway, Nini usually stayed at her designated cabin post, the small one with the double decker bunks. She would secret herself well back comfortably on a pillow in the dark with her fur coat pulled tightly about her. To Nini, the engines were a deafening roar which were only good for sleeping.

Once in a slip or at anchor, Nini always joined the captain and first mate for a tete-a-tete in the main cabin. At bedtime, all retired to the captain's cabin for a menage-a-kitty replete with warm nose nudges, kisses and purrs.

Her special gourmet delights still await her discerning palate. Nini's one regret was that her paw shape prevented her from joining with the captain, crew and guests in afternoon Happy Hour libations.

She is sorely missed both as a fearless seafaring soul and fastidious and loving lady at home in Wilton. So, beat the drum slowly and drape the crepe darkly as we honor this elegant kitty, Ninian Jones.

In lieu of flowers, please send a donation to Animals in Distress Inc., Wilton Town Hall, Wilton 06897 in her name.

BETTY JONES
Westport Road, Oct. 21

**Remembering the BETTY-GENE's second mate**

Doug and I enjoying ourselves on the afterdeck

## SON, JEFF JONES:
Even as a child, our son Jeff was musically an artistic shaker and mover. At Wilton High School, it was very difficult to get him to leave the school's recording studio, where he would remain into the wee hours of the night instead of coming home to bed.

In the fall of 1973, Jeff began his freshman year at my alma mater, Sarah Lawrence College. Since I had enjoyed my years at this innovative progressive school, Doug and I thought that Jeff, who in many ways is very much like me, would feel likewise. In addition, Doug was on the Sarah Lawrence College Board of Trustees, which was helpful in every way. At Sarah Lawrence, Jeff continued his interest in recording music.

After years of accumulating experience locally, Jeff moved to New York. His first big break came when Wynton Marsalis, Willie Nelson and Bill Cosby all recognized his true worth by engaging him to mix the sound for their upcoming CD's.

Marsalis, who was the Artistic Director of "Jazz at Lincoln Center," then appointed Jeff as the Center's chief sound engineer.

In 2009, Jeff won a coveted GRAMMY Award for co-producing the best contemporary blues album. Today, he is much in demand and enjoys the work he loves with great passion.

**Proud Mother with Jeff on his wedding day (1990)**

## DAUGHTER, JANET JONES SHIPP:

When Janet was in her senior year at Wilton High School, she started thinking about colleges and soon realized that it would be in her best interest to decide which subject she would like to major in. Janet seemed to enjoy both math and science, so I asked her, "What about engineering?" To get a better understanding of what becoming an engineer would entail, she questioned her father extensively and decided to give it a try. Accepted at Middlebury College in Vermont, she enrolled in their cooperative engineering program which Middlebury shared with Georgia Institute of Technology in Atlanta.

Proud mother with Janet on her wedding day (1984)

Her zeal to become an engineer diminished by degrees the longer she studied the discipline. With our approval, Janet switched her major from engineering to her secret love, modern dance. As is often said, "The acorn never falls far from the tree." Like her Mom, she also enjoyed singing and joined the Middlebury College Choir. Janet was born with a good sounding voice but without a vibrato. As luck would have it, its absence proved to be a distinct asset. The Vermont Symphony was looking high and low for a boy soprano to be their soloist in a performance of Benjamin Britten's *Chichester Psalms.* A young boy's voice is usually a straight, vibrato-less sound. Janet possessed just what they were looking for. After many rehearsals, the Middlebury Choir, with Janet Jones as soloist was given the honor of performing this difficult music in concert with the Vermont Symphony Orchestra. She sang triumphantly.

Janet graduated from Middlebury cum laude in 1979. Because of her natural abilities and the newly learned dance discipline which she perfected at Middlebury, she auditioned for and was welcomed into the Alvin Ailey Professional Dance Troupe. Going to see her dance at New York's City Center was a wonderful experience for both Doug and I. Evidently her father's business genes exerted a stronger career pull than we anticipated because Janet left Ailey and returned to Connecticut where she earned an MBA from the University of Bridgeport. She did this while working as an operations director for the internationally known Tauck Tours. After a time, Janet moved on to Glencore Ltd., making quite a name for herself at this commodities trading firm in Stamford, Connecticut.

## 50TH WEDDING ANNIVERSARY:

In 2004, our daughter Janet and her husband Nate secretly decided to celebrate our 50th Wedding Anniversary, my 75th and Doug's 80th Birthday by throwing a gigantic surprise party at their home here in Wilton. On that special night by the time we arrived, the party was in full swing. Every window was ablaze with light and in the dark, we could just about make out that cars lined both sides of the road. As we opened the front door to walk in, we were greeted by a thunderous cheer of welcome from all those present. What a supreme joy it was to see and greet those whom we have long held dear from the past to present. Many family members and dear friends were there including my old boyfriend Henry (and his wife Ethel). I heard it said that when I was first introduced to him, I was only a few months old. During a visit, I had been momentarily laid down to nap by my mother on his parents bed. We've been fast friends ever since that time.

**Our 50th wedding anniversary**
**Plus my 75th & Doug's 80th birthday (2004)**

There were many speeches given honoring us before dinner. When I in turn, was asked to take center stage, I said, "No matter how many years Doug and I are married, there will always be something new to discover about each other, like the idea of removing over time all of the seven veils, as found in Strauss' opera, *Salome*."

# Finale

## HEARING PROBLEMS:

When engaged by the Metropolitan Opera to cover Leonie Rysanek as the Empress in Strauss's _Die Frau Ohne Shatten,_ Walter Taussig, a well known Met assistant conductor in the German repertoire, coached me in learning this difficult role. As we worked, I began to feel an ever increasing need to get my hearing tested professionally. Taussig suggested I go to his audiologist, who then confirmed my greatest fear. I did indeed have the beginnings of a hearing deficit. At our next coaching session together, Walter ventured cautiously to suggest that I consider purchasing a hearing aid called the Diva, which he personally swore by and had found to be magically helpful. In his heavy German accent he quipped, "Now my hearing is so good that I can actually catch my colleagues in their mistakes." Since an operatic soprano is sometimes referred to as a Diva, which translated into English means Divine, so, following his suggestion, I purchased the Diva and instantly became a Double Diva. I am one and I have another in my ear. However, I certainly did not want anyone to know of my predicament. After being helped into my costume in preparation for a performance, I would usually wait until the costumers had finished dressing me completely including putting on my elaborate make-up and wig. Then just before going on stage, I would surreptitiously slip my precious Diva into my ear canal and smugly smile, thinking to myself that no one will ever be the wiser.

## REFLECTIONS:

At the end of performances, when the last strains of the orchestra faded away and the stage darkened after the curtain descended, I began to fear, because of my hearing loss, that my operatic career could come to a similar slow motion fate. Unfortunately, what I had anticipated became a reality. As time passed, my hearing continued deteriorating to the point where I was finally forced to give up singing opera. My last full performance was in 1982, singing the role of Odabella in Verdi's _Attila_ with the New York City Opera. What I did not realize was that over the years I had positively touched many hearts and lives when performing and that there would come a time when the world began to return the favor. Sure enough, after my retirement inquiring phone calls to our Connecticut home began to pick up in frequency. My voice teaching responsibilities soon explosively doubled in size to 40 hours a week and many organizations began begging me to sing locally and lend my voice and presence to their special occasions.

Around this same time, I began to silently reflect on how I happened to enter the rarefied world of opera despite my major interest in college having been painting and sculpture. I studied music for only a short while. Now that my singing career had essentially ended, I finally revealed my most hidden secret to the world, "I can't sight read music." Conquering sight singing had completely escaped me. I came to the conclusion that it would always be difficult for me to read music without hearing it first. Over the years, I learned the opera vocal techniques and repertoire by studying with various voice teachers and coaches but never sight singing. I shared my dismay with conductor Henry Holt when I was about to sing my first Aida with the Seattle Opera Company. He calmed my fears by countering with the positive comment, "When you perform and you do an unbelievably good job both musically and dramatically, as you have in the past, no one will ever think of asking you, 'But can you read music?' The strength of your excellently creative musicianship and acting will more than compensate for any ill conceived lack or uneasy feeling of inadequacy on your part. When your performance is over, a thunderous applause will always accompany your many gracious bows."

## CONNECTICUT ARTS AWARD:

The crowning moment of my totally unexpected career occurred when the Connecticut Commission on the Arts presented me with its coveted 1986 Arts Award at a "black tie" dinner held at the Wadsworth Atheneum in Hartford. At that time, a 30 minute television special on my life was shown on Connecticut Public TV throughout the state. Past winners include the celebrated contralto Marian Anderson, fellow Wilton resident jazz

**Our Wilton, CT. house**
**Connecticut Arts Award in 1986**

pianist Dave Brubeck and the noted historian Barbara Tuchman.

After I was introduced at the dinner and my artistic triumphs enumerated, I stepped up to the microphone draped in my carefully chosen bright red full length gown. The gold award medal of honor was ceremoniously hung around my neck by the Governor and, as I proudly accepted it, I said teasingly into the mike, "Of course you know ---- I'd rather sing than speak." A muffled titter spread through the audience. After it died down, I continued my high spirited, spontaneous acceptance speech.

A few weeks before this event, a crew of 20 arrived at our house to begin taping my television special which took almost

10 hours to complete. The first thing they did was to rearrange the furniture. The director made sure that the television audience would be able to see the paintings and sculptures I had done and were in the background of every scene during the interview. My accompanist, Don Comrie, then played the introduction to every one's favorite I had chosen to sing, Gershwin's "Summertime." He continued on to supportively accompany me as I taught a short demonstration voice lesson to one of my students.

In order to further publicize the event, the Commission on the Arts retained a special photographer to capture still pictures of me during my television interview. Shortly afterwards the pictures appeared in feature articles throughout Connecticut. This kind of hoopla continued for years after the elegant Wadsworth Atheneum event, making me feel greatly loved and wanted as the distinguished singer I had always hoped to become.

### UNEXPECTED SURPRISE COMMUNICATIONS:

On October 31, 2007 (Halloween), I received an e-mail from a man named David Shengold that caused my heart to become totally twitterpated. It concerned a New York City Opera performance of _Un Ballo in Maschera_ that I sang and he attended as a schoolboy on April 11, 1976. Although many years had passed since this particular performance, Shengold, who had become a reviewer for and contributor to _Opera News_ and other music publications, was so impressed by my performance as Amelia that he felt it helped him to discover his life's calling as a writer and reviewer.

Then on February 15, 2010, I received a hurried telephone call from one of my voice students. He said that while trolling e-Bay, he had come across a "Betty Jones Live Opera Recording" that was up for bid and that the bidding period would be closing in a few hours. Doug immediately got on his computer and was able to purchase this live recording of the _Un Ballo in Maschera_ I had sung on April 20, 1976. Once it

213

was in my possession, I was transfixed with pride and joy as I listened to it the first time.

Subj: **To Dr. Betty Jones**
Date: Wednesday, October 31, 2007 11:06:17 PM
From: shengold@yahoo.com
To: eugjones@aol.com

Dear Dr. Jones--

By complete coincidence I came across two excellent web articles describing your life and career, and was most gratified to read them.

When I was a schoolboy, I bought my first subscription to the New York City Opera. One of the things on it that gave me particular pleasure was the UN BALLO IN MASCHERA of April 11, 1976, in which you sang Amelia (opposite Ermanno Mauro, Richard Fredricks, Glenys Fowles and Frances Bible, led by Julius Rudel). This remains my favorite Verdi score.

Where I was sitting in the Third Ring there was an old New York couple next to me who were praising your performance after Act One. A very gracious lady turned to us and said with (justifiable) pride, "That's my daughter up there!

I also remember that there was an elderly emigree lady I ran into regularly that used to regale me with stories of the fantastic casts she had heard in Vienna in the 1920s. She had heard the great Maria Nemeth in BALLO, she said before the show, kind of implying that no one was going to live up to her memories of Maria Nemeth! But even she, when I found her in the second intermission, said approvingly: "She hass a gut pair of pipes!!"

That was the only time I had the luck to hear you. I went off to college in Massacheetts and grad schoool in California and by the time I moved back East you had retired. So I was very glad to learn about all your activities.

These days, as it happens, I am a reviewer for and contributor to OPERA NEWS and OPERA magazines. So those early memorable performances really sent me on a lifelong journey.

Wishing you and your family all the best--

David Shengold

**Email from David Shengold, opera critic**

The Music In My Life

BETTY JONES BALLO IN MASCHERA 1976 LIVE OPERA
RECORDING

opera_king ( 432 ☆ )

Item condition:   Very Good

Time left:   6h 27m 6s (Feb 15, 2010 18:15:36 PST)

Bid history:   13 bids

Current bid:   **US $46.50**

Item specifics - Music: CDs

| Genre: | Classical | Duration: | Album or EP |
| Sub-Genre: | Opera | Condition: | Very Good |
| Special Attributes: | -- | | |

Seller's description

From my personal collection of private recordings, you are bidding on audio CDs of a live opera recording featuring the Great African American Soprano BETTY JONES. Jones enjoyed a relatively brief but major career immediately after her opera career began. She came to opera later in life than most, but arrived with a very impressive voice form the start. She was very tall with a Hollywood figure and a Verdi Soprano voice with an easy top. Live recordings of Betty Jones are hard to come by, but here she is in a 1976 UN BALLO IN MASCHERA, recorded in very good, up-close, non-broadcast sound. Jones is at her best in this difficult role, and is joined by a young Ermanno Mauro in top form. The recording is complete on 2 CDs, has complete tracking, is on-pitch and comes in a jewel box (overseas packages will be sent without the jewel box).

NOTICE: After a title search of the Library of Congress Copyright records, no copyright exists on this material; therefore making this program Public Domain. This material does not violate any copyright laws, and is in compliance with Ebay's policies regarding Public Domain material.

**Un Ballo in Maschera**

NYCO 4/20/76

Amelia-   Betty Jones

Ulrica- Muriel Costa-Greenspon

Riccardo-   Ermanno Mauro

Oscar- Gianna Rolandi

Renato- Pablo Elvira

Conductor- Julius Rudel

http://cgi.ebay.com/ws/eBayISAPI.dll?ViewItem&item=260550576932&si=R4mbTzFU...   2010-02-17

**Ebay listing - Betty Jones Live Opera Recording**

## FINAL THOUGHTS:

Writing this book has afforded me a fabulous opportunity to remember my past triumphs. THANK YOU beloved audience and friends for giving me the opportunity to sing leading roles in opera companies around the world. Interestingly enough, my study of painting and sculpture at Sarah Lawrence College helped me immeasurably to teach myself to visualize, through meditation in picture form and color, the plot, situations and characters of the operas I was about to play. This led to far greater dramatic authenticity of the roles I was to sing. In order to bring back the past and write this book, I have learned to draw heavily on this precious self taught gift of visualization. Like watching closed circuit television, it has brought me poignant joy (even at the age of 84 years) to again see myself and my colleagues in costume in the spotlight on the stage making beautiful music together. I hear the audience clap, I take my bow gracefully ------ and ------ SMILE!

# Acknowledgments

Johnny Rose, a wonderful pianist as well as a Reiki Master first suggested I consider writing a book which would give an inside look at entering the difficult world of being an opera singer when past the age of 40. My husband Doug thought it was a great idea and encouraged me to attend a writing class he had read about which was being formed at our local Wilton, Connecticut Senior Center. In the class, I had to write a 2 or 3 page story each week which was reviewed by other participants.

Besides Johnny, I would like to thank Magdalen Livesey, our senior class leader, Connie Tate, Bill Ziegler, plus all my fellow writing class members for their wonderful comradeship and very helpful comments on some of my early writings. In addition, Lois Alcosser, Maureen Maguire and Lois Hutzler all assisted in just getting me started. Former Connecticut neighbors and close friends Charlotte Hoffman in Durham, North Carolina and Neysa Hebbard in Portland, Oregon plus Alcosser reviewed many initial drafts and provided continued encouragement.

Finally, it was Doug who assembled and catalogued the many aspects of my career and Bill Ziegler who provided the very best in the final editing. THANK YOU ALL!

# About The Author

Betty Jones, a Sarah Lawrence College graduate, majored in art. After singing in a church choir for many years, at the age of 41 she embarked on an international operatic career. Her first appearance was with the Boston Opera Company in 1971. Other major companies include: New York City Opera, San Francisco, Chicago Lyric, Seattle, Chautauqua, Washington, etc., as well as companies in Italy, Germany and England. During Betty's career, she has sung many of the principal soprano roles including Aida, Tosca, Turandot, Countess (*Le Nozze di Figaro*), Leonore (*Fidelio*), Amelia (*Un Ballo in Maschera*), Senta (*Der Fliegende Hollander*), Odabella (*Attila*), Eva (*Die Meistersinger*), Abigaille (*Nabucco*), plus various roles in the complete Wagner *Ring Cycle.*

She really made her mark by going on at the last minute performing leading soprano roles for indisposed singers. One of these was a 1978 *Oberon* performance at Carnegie

Hall opposite world famous tenor Nicolai Gedda. The next day, the entire New York opera world was talking about Betty Jones with astonishment and admiration.

Mother of two and grandmother of three, she lives in Wilton, Connecticut where in 2014 she and her husband, Eugene D. Jones, celebrated their 60th wedding anniversary.